Insight Meditation

Insight Meditation

The Practice of Freedom

Joseph Goldstein

Shambhala
Boston & London
1993

Shambhala Publications, Inc.
Horticultural Hall
300 Massachusetts Avenue
Boston, Massachusetts 02115

9   8   7   6   5   4   3   2   1

First Edition
Printed in the United States of America on acid-free paper ♾
Distributed in the United States by Random House, Inc.,
and in Canada by Random House of Canada Ltd

Library of Congress Cataloging-in-Publication Data

Goldstein, Joseph, 1944–
Insight meditation: the practice of freedom /
Joseph Goldstein. — 1st ed.
p.   cm.
Includes index.   ISBN 0-87773-895-5
1. Spiritual life—Buddhism.   I. Title.
BQ5675.G65   1993   93-21830
294.3'444—dc20   CIP

Dedicated to those
whose generosity and love of the Dharma
have made possible so many things

The birds have vanished into the sky,
and now the last cloud drains away.

We sit together, the mountain and me,
Until only the mountain remains.

—Li Po

Contents

Contents

Preface

May 1965. Thailand Ten, one of the first Peace Corps groups, drink champagne at thirty thousand feet above the Pacific, toasting the West going East. Because I am not yet twenty-one, Pan Am will not serve me. What I know about Buddhism would not fill one of those tiny, stemmed plastic glasses: a smiling man with a big belly, an idea of calm, nonattachment, breathing through all things.

July 1974. At summer session, Naropa Institute, Boulder, Colorado, a Buddhist Woodstock celebrates the East coming West. My initiation as Dharma teacher in America. In the midst of the exhilaration, people wanting to know. I feel the wind gathering, lifting us all, and I think, "This is the beginning of something."

January 1993. A generation later, the teachings of the Buddha blow steadily, gently through our Western culture. A three-month retreat ends, our eighteenth since 1975. One hundred people walk out into the world, some smiling calmly, others on fire with the truth of their experience. My blue computer screen shines with their questions into winter's early night.

The Buddha's Lion Roar calls us all to awaken. If we know how to look, we discover wisdom and compassion, the true nature of our mind. Inspired by this possibility, many of us have been learning to look, to question, to see for ourselves.

Discovery is the first step.

And the next? His Holiness the Sixteenth Karmapa of Tibet expressed it very simply: "We have to do what we know." To free our mind, we put discovery into practice.

Many Westerners have been practicing Buddhist insight meditation for nearly twenty years. Some sit daily. Some come for weekend or nine-day courses. Others do three-month retreats, or many three-month retreats. Some do even longer ones. Within that range there is every possibility.

What follows touches on a wide range of topics repeatedly raised by students of the Dharma. These practical, incisive, often compelling questions gave birth to this book.

Joseph Goldstein
Barre, Massachusetts
January 1993

Acknowledgments

I wish to express my gratitude to the many people who helped make this book possible:

Eric Kolvig, whose stellar editing skills, painstaking efforts, and lucidity of mind show on every page;

Sharon Salzberg, Michele McDonald Smith, Steven Smith, Carol Wilson, and Steve Armstrong, my three-month-retreat teaching colleagues, all of whom provide the grist, support, and friendship that has nourished my understanding over many years;

Devi Harris, who with love and wit offered a room with a view, a notebook computer, and very good pasta;

Kedar, for countless hours of bracing Dharma combat and much good humor in the process;

Kendra Crossen, Andy Cooper, and DeAnna Lunden, whose editing suggestions were always helpful;

Anasuya Weil, for her steady and careful transcribing;

The staff at IMS, for their generous service to the Dharma;

And the many people whose questions gave birth to this whole endeavor.

May the merit of this book be dedicated to the happiness and liberation of all beings.

One
What Is the Path?

The Dharma

"Done is what had to be done."

This phrase, found so often in Buddhist texts, always inspires me. It appears in many "songs of enlightenment," words exclaimed by women and men at the moment of their liberation. These words bring me joy because they are reminders that we can actually walk the path of freedom to the end. It will be a wonderful moment when we sing that song, "Done is what had to be done."

But questions may haunt us: "Is it possible to awaken? It may have been possible for the Buddha, but is it possible for me? Can I really do it?" We can, if we know the way.

We practice the Dharma in order to understand that way, in order to be free. That is the heart of all the effort we make, because from freedom come connectedness, compassion, lovingkindness, and peace. The word *Dharma* in Sanskrit, or *Dhamma* in Pali, is a huge umbrella term with many different meanings. Among others, it means the truth of the way things are. It means the specific elements of experience and the natural laws that govern that experience. *Dharma* also refers to the teachings of the Buddha and to the paths of practice that lead to awakening. So Dharma is all-inclusive. Everything is the Dharma; everything follows its own lawful nature.

The Buddha saw with such clarity how different states of mind and courses of action lead to different results. Unwholesome mind states have certain consequences. Wholesome mind states have results of their own. As we begin to understand the truth of how things are, we see for ourselves what brings suffering in our lives, and what brings happiness and freedom.

In true spiritual undertakings there is no compulsion. The Buddha laid out a comprehensive map of reality. When we understand the map well, we can choose freely which direction we want to take. It is simple. If we want to be happy, and if we understand the causes for happiness, then, when we cultivate those causes, happiness follows.

We can make such choices because Dharma is the reality of natural law, of how things work. If our lives unfolded randomly, with no physical or moral laws operating, then we could not influence the direction of our lives at all; we would simply be subject to the winds of chaos. Although at first our mind might feel like a whirlwind of activity, the amazing path of Dharma practice helps us begin to sort things out. We establish some stability and focus in our mind and see which elements in it lead to greater peace, which to greater suffering. All of it—both the peace and the suffering—happens lawfully. Freedom lies in the wisdom to choose.

As we walk the way of awareness, we see that the deepest purpose we all have is to perfect the qualities of our heart and mind. The spiritual path transforms our consciousness, purifying it of greed, hatred, ignorance, fear, envy, jealousy—those forces that create suffering in us and in the world.

We all share this most fundamental purpose of freedom. It is the universal potential of the mind itself. In my early years of practice in India, I studied with Munindra-ji, one of my teachers, in Bodh Gaya, the place where the Buddha awakened. Bodh Gaya is a small village with many beautiful temples, and as Munindra-ji and I would walk together through the village, he would often point out very simple village people who had been his students. Many of them had attained different stages of enlightenment.

Seeing these people encouraged me, because judging from outward appearances, you would never guess their spiritual attainments. They looked like simple village folk going about their business. I came to appreciate, firsthand, the often-stated truth that realization does not depend on social or educational background. Everyone shares the basic commonality of being alive, of having a mind and heart. Our task is to awaken and purify this mind-heart for the benefit of all.

Understanding this task, this path, gives a context in which to hold and measure each of our actions. Does this action we are about to perform—any action—help us awaken, or does it hinder us? In all our different life situations we can practice purifying our mind. When we know and connect with the path of freedom, and when we commit ourselves to it, no matter what, then beyond any doubt we will one day exclaim our own song of enlightenment: "Done is what had to be done."

Fear of Enlightenment

Meditators sometimes report that fear of liberation holds them back in their practice; as they proceed into uncharted territory, fear of the unknown becomes an obstacle to surrender. But this is not really fear of enlightenment. It is rather fear of *ideas about* enlightenment. We all have notions about freedom: dissolving in a great burst of light, or in a great cosmic flash. The mind might invent many different images of the experience of liberation. Sometimes our ego creates images of its own death that frighten us.

Liberation means letting go of suffering. Do you fear the prospect of being free from greed? Do you fear being free from anger or delusion? Probably not. Liberation means freeing ourselves from those qualities in the mind that torment and limit us. So freedom is not something magical or mysterious. It does not make us weird. Enlightenment means purifying our mind and letting go of those things that cause so much suffering in our lives. It is very down-to-earth.

Imagine holding on to a hot burning coal. You would not fear letting go of it. In fact, once you noticed that you were holding on, you would probably drop it quickly. But we often do not recognize how we hold on to suffering. It seems to hold on to us. This is our practice: becoming aware of how suffering arises in our mind and of how we become identified with it, and learning to let it go. We learn through simple and direct observation, seeing the process over and over again until we understand.

When the Buddha described his teaching in the most concise way, he said that he taught one thing and one thing only: suffering and the end of suffering. Understanding this reality for ourself frees our mind and opens more fully the possibilities for compassionate action in the world.

Intelligence and Progress

Awakening is for everybody. I think it is fortunate that progress on the path does not depend on the level of one's intelligence. Coming to understand this fact was a great opening for me during my years of training to be a teacher.

When I was in India training with my teacher, Munindra-ji, I sat in on many of his interviews with yogis to watch how he taught. After some of the interviews, he would describe which meditation subjects were suitable for different individuals. Once he said, "Oh yes, this one is suitable for intelligent people, and this one for stupid people." I had an immediate, strong reaction to this categorization. Because of a certain middle-class, Western conditioning, I was offended that anyone would be considered stupid.

It was freeing to learn that for spiritual practice there is no preference regarding intelligence. Some people are intelligent, and others are not. According to the teaching, if you are intelligent you do one thing, and if you are dull you do another. The *Visuddhimagga (The Path of Purification),* a compendium of much of the Buddha's teachings, describes different meditation subjects and indicates for whom each is best suited.

Over the years I have come to appreciate both the obvious strengths intelligence provides and some of its tremendous dangers. We all know people who become strongly identified with, and attached to, their intelligence. It can become a big ego trap, harmful to oneself or others. Intelligence can also be a great blessing, providing invaluable clarity. For me it was important to learn that many other qualities of mind reflect nobility and beauty of character much more than intelligence. Generosity, love, compassion, or devotion do not depend on a high IQ.

One of my favorite stories from the Buddha's time tells about a disciple of the Buddha who was very dull. His brother, another disciple, was an *arhat,* fully enlightened, and was also very smart. The dullard had been inspired by the teachings and had been ordained as a monk. He had the sweetest heart, but his mind was really slow. Because he was slow, his brother gave him as his practice a four-line verse of the Buddha's teachings to memorize.

The dullard struggled and struggled to learn one line. Then, as he was trying to learn the second line, it pushed out the first. One line was all his mind could hold. This struggle went on and on; he simply did not have the intelligence to do it. His arhat brother finally gave up and said, "This is hopeless. You had better leave the order of monks." The poor dullard was totally dejected. He felt so sad, because his heart was devoted to the Dharma.

As the dullard was walking back to his village, feeling very low, the Buddha, knowing what had happened, came and walked by his side. He stroked the poor dullard's head and consoled him by giving him a practice exactly suitable to his condition. "Here's a meditation subject for you. Take this white handkerchief and stand out in the hot sun and rub it." That was the whole meditation.

So the dullard took the handkerchief, went out in the sun, and began to rub it. Slowly the handerchief started to become dirty with the sweat from his hand. As that happened, memories awakened in him of previous lifetimes of practice, when he had seen impurities coming from his body. As he continued to watch the soiled handkerchief, a profound dispassion arose and his mind opened. He became fully enlightened. It is said that as he became enlightened, intelligence and all the traditional psychic powers came to him, in addition to deep understanding of the Dharma. The story then ends by describing some good-humored psychic tricks the former dullard played on his surprised brother.

I feel great affection for the dullard.

One Taste

Is enlightenment gradual or is it sudden? Whole schools of Buddhism have grown up around this issue. But it has always seemed to me that liberation is both sudden and gradual, that there is no polarity between the two.

Enlightenment is always sudden. It is grace; when the conditions are right, it happens. But the path leading up to that moment is gradual. We practice, we create the field, we prepare the ground, and the mind eventually opens suddenly and spontaneously. Then again, after sudden awakening can come a gradual cultivation and ripening of the enlightened mind.

The Buddha declared straightforwardly that our mind in its natural state is pure but that it is obscured by visiting defilements. In one of his discourses he said, "The mind is radiant, shining, glowing forth; but it is stained by the defilements that visit it. The mind is radiant, shining, glowing forth, and from the uprooting of defilements that visit it, it is freed."

Techniques may vary, but the essential teachings of the Buddha — on the nature of suffering and the realization of freedom — are found in all the Buddhist traditions. Countless forms have evolved in all the places where the Dharma has flourished: India, Burma, Thailand, Tibet, China, Japan, Korea, Sri Lanka, Cambodia, Vietnam, and elsewhere. Munindra-ji told me long ago that he was familiar with over fifty techniques of insight meditation in Burma alone.

Do not become attached to the idea that there is only one right way or technique of practicing the Dharma. Freedom and compassion are the reference points for all practice. Everything else is skillful means. There are many experiences along the way. As soon as we take a stand any place at all, thinking "this is it," we have already overshot the great jewel of emptiness, creating yet another sectarian view.

One of my teachers voiced what I think is true for all traditions, practices, techniques, and views. He said, "Unless a practice cools the fires of greed, aversion, and ignorance it is worthless." This is the measure of everything we do.

What is truly wonderful about the Dharma in the West is the

opportunity for practitioners of all traditions to meet and learn from one another. Each of the great traditions—Theravada, Mahayana, and Vajrayana (Tibetan Buddhism)—has so much to offer. As the Buddha said, "The Dharma has one taste, the taste of freedom."

And for all of us practice is the key. There is a wonderful story of Milarepa, the great Tibetan yogi. It seems that at the end of his life Milarepa took his foremost disciple to a remote mountainside in order to transmit the most secret teachings. With great reverence and devotion the disciple requested the transmission. Milarepa then bent over, exposed his backside, and pointed to the leatherlike calluses that had developed from his years of sitting.

As individuals we will have different cycles as our practice unfolds. There are times when you might have a lot of energy for intensive, silent meditation retreats that can help stabilize strong awareness and open new levels of insight. At a certain point, however, you might find yourself losing energy for such intensity in practice. This waning in the cycle might come after a few years, a few months, or even, at first, after a few days of intensive practice. When it comes depends on each person's level of development and particular life situation.

I knew one retreatant who had been practicing in Asia for several months. His practice had reached a certain level of maturity, but for some reason he could not make any further progress. When our teacher asked him about conditions at home, he spoke about a compelling desire to see his family again. Our teacher advised him to return home for a visit. After seeing his family, his mind was cleared of that obstacle, and when he came again to practice, he finished that particular course of training.

Be wary of holding a fixed model of how your practice should proceed. At times you may be drawn to investigate your mind in a secluded retreat situation. At other times, you may not feel this need for solitude. Just follow the rhythm of the cycle in a simple, natural way. If liberation is the central aspiration of your life, periods of intensive meditation practice can be of inestimable value. They generate tremendous energy, power, and insight. But there are also cycles of living actively in the world, developing generosity, morality, truthfulness, and compassion, qualities more easily expressed in daily life than in retreat. Then in turn these great strengths of mind will further empower your intensive meditation.

Four Noble Truths

As the teachings of the Buddha spread throughout Asia and the world, many schools of interpretation arose, each with its own emphasis, metaphysics, and skillful means. Although the different traditions may disagree about some points of Dharma, one formulation of the teachings remains the central jewel common to them all: the Four Noble Truths.

The Buddha described the First Noble Truth as the truth of suffering. The word *dukkha* in Pali has a wide range of meanings, including suffering, insecurity, and unsatisfactoriness. The Buddha awakened, without fear or self-pity, to the reality of suffering in life. He recognized the problems of suffering very clearly: the pain of birth, old age, death, sorrow, pain, grief, despair, association with the unloved, separation from the loved, not getting what we want—all this is dukkha. As we investigate the nature of conditioned phenomena on increasingly deep and subtle levels, we begin to see their inherently unsatisfying nature.

We all know that painful feelings in our bodies or in our minds are suffering. But we can also understand this truth of dukkha when we become aware of the momentariness of experience. No experience, no matter how wonderful, will bring us a deep and lasting satisfaction, precisely because it is always changing. The continuous flow of phenomena often reminds me of water going over the lip of a high waterfall. The water is endlessly falling away—*whissssh!*—without stopping, without rest. That is the nature of all experience.

In addition, the Buddha described a third kind of suffering very graphically in the Fire Sermon: "The eye is burning, the ear is burning . . . the body . . . the mind . . . burning with what? Burning with the fire of greed, the fire of aversion, the fire of ignorance."

We find it hard to open to the truth of suffering because we are conditioned to seek refuge in conventional ways. We seek our refuge and happiness in pleasurable things, in things that are themselves transitory. Often we do not make the necessary effort to stop, to open, to sensitize ourselves to what is really going on.

The wonderful paradox about the truth of suffering is that the more we open to it and understand it, the lighter and freer our mind becomes. Our mind becomes more spacious, more open, and happier as we move past our avoidance and denial to see what is true. We become less driven by compulsive desires and addictions, because we see clearly the nature of things as they are.

But it is not enough simply to see and understand the suffering in our lives. The Second Noble Truth recognizes its causes. What are the causes of suffering? The Pali word is *kilesa,* which means afflictive emotions, the torments of the mind, such as greed, envy, hatred, anger, fear. These states and others torment us and create suffering.

Kilesas manifest on different levels. Sometimes they are so strong that they can cause what one Buddhist monk from Burma translated as "outrageous behavior": killing, stealing, sexual misconduct, causing great harm to oneself and others. The force of these kilesas is so obvious when we look at what is happening all over the world: murder, rape, torture, starvation, national hatreds. All this suffering has its roots in people's minds, in our own mind.

We can abandon this level of suffering when we have a commitment to ethical precepts, to nonharming behavior. The Buddha taught five training precepts as a great protection from these kinds of harmful acts: not killing, not stealing, not committing sexual misconduct, not lying, and not taking intoxicants that cloud the mind. Imagine how different the world would be if everyone followed just part of *one* of these precepts—not to kill other human beings.

A middle level of kilesas is those unwholesome states of mind that bring about actions of speech or mind that are somewhat less impactful. And the subtlest level of kilesas is called latent defilements, or latent afflictive tendencies. These are not present in the moment but have the potential to arise if they are given the appropriate circumstances. We can see these latencies at work when people are put in situations of overwhelming stress and commit actions they might not normally even consider.

The Buddha placed great emphasis on uprooting one particular defilement in order to abandon the causes of suffering. This kilesa, considered the most dangerous, is the strong belief in and view of some permanent "self." As long as our mind is afflicted by that wrong view, by that incorrect perception, of things, it leads us on to perform many other kinds of unwholesome actions. If we have a mistaken notion of "I," then we need to defend it and gratify it, and thus many of our actions begin to revolve around this wrong view. The writer Wei Wu Wei succinctly expressed this root kilesa's delusive effect: "It is like a dog barking up a tree that isn't there."

Meditation purifies the mind of this most deeply conditioned kilesa, which has caused so much suffering in our lives and which is the basic misperception of our existence. Through the power of mindful awareness, we get a sense, a taste, of what selflessness—absence of self—means. We understand it, not theoretically or conceptually, but in the experienced freedom of the moment.

Such liberating understanding is not new. It goes back to the time of the Buddha and to countless Buddhas before him. This understanding is the nature of the Dharma itself. It is also expressed in the wisdom of many people of different cultures. A fourteenth-century Japanese samurai wrote:

> I have no parents
> > I make the heavens and earth my parents
> I have no home
> > I make awareness my home
> I have no life or death
> > I make the tides of breathing my life and death
> I have no divine power
> > I make honesty my divine power
> I have no friends
> > I make my mind my friend
> I have no enemy
> > I make carelessness my enemy
> I have no armor
> > I make benevolence my armor
> I have no castle
> > I make immovable-mind my castle
> I have no sword
> > I make absence of self my sword.

We are all samurai, making "absence of self" our sword. That sword of wisdom cuts through ignorance, cuts through delusion.

The First Noble Truth teaches the truth of suffering and its different levels. The practitioner who understands the Second Noble Truth recognizes and abandons the causes of suffering, and weakens and uproots the afflictions of the mind, particularly the view of self.

The Third Noble Truth teaches that there can be an end of suffering, a putting down of the burden. We glimpse the end of suffering at different times in our practice. We can taste this freedom in just the moment when a kilesa vanishes. When we are caught by the afflictive emotions, we feel tight, burning, contracted; and in the moment when we let go of that identification, our mind is released. Right in that moment we have a taste of freedom, a taste of the end of suffering. This freedom is real; it is in our own experience; it is not just some nice idea. Every time we become aware of a thought, as opposed to being lost in a thought, we experience that opening of the mind.

A familiar experience of this release comes when we go to the movies, become totally absorbed in the story, and then walk outside. A kind of reality shift happens, a little jolt of awakening: "Oh, that was just a movie!" But how much are we lost in the nonstop movies of our mind? Every moment when we are mindfully aware of what is happening becomes a moment of awakening from our own story. "Oh, yes, that was just a thought. It is not the big drama that I believed it to be." This is a moment of opening.

We experience the truth of the end of suffering in another way at that stage of meditation practice called "equanimity about formations." A mind suffused with equanimity is poised and balanced with whatever may be arising in its experience. We feel soft and spacious as things come and go; an equanimous mind does not move reactively at all. This state is likened to the mind of a fully enlightened being. So even before we have realized complete liberation, we can still experience this place of peace.

We also experience the truth of the end of suffering by opening to the end of all conditioned phenomena—the realization of the unconditioned, the unborn.

The Fourth Noble Truth of the Buddha's awakening gives the full development of the path leading to liberation. This path of practice is direct and straightforward, although it takes tremendous perseverance and commitment. The path of practice consists of three trainings. First we train in morality, in nonharming. If we try to practice meditation without the foundation of goodwill to ourselves and others, it is like trying to row across a river without first untying the boat; our efforts, no matter how strenuous, will not bear fruit. We need to practice and refine our ability to live honestly and with integrity.

In the second training, we develop energy, concentration, and mindfulness. These are the meditative and life tools that enable us to awaken. Without them we simply act out the patterns of our conditioning.

These two trainings are the foundation for the third, which is the emergence of wisdom. Wisdom is the clear seeing of the impermanent, conditioned nature of all phenomena, knowing that whatever arises has the nature to cease. When we see this impermanence deeply, we no longer cling; and when we no longer cling, we come to the end of suffering.

Signposts

Nothing we do creates the unconditioned. Everything arising in this mind and body is a conditioned phenomenon. All elements of experience arise and pass, conditioned by causes. The unconditioned is uncaused, unborn, beyond all arising and passing. The unconditioned is there. It has always been there. It is not something created in time; it is not something created at all. We could call it the ground of being, or the ultimate reality, or nirvana, or the unborn—there are countless names for it. And just as a path that goes to a mountain does not cause the mountain, the path of practice leads us to this highest freedom, but does not cause it.

What we do is walk on this path, and when the conditions are right, the mind opens. That opening can happen at any time. There are some signposts along this path that are common to many, although people can also open in many different ways.

The Buddha often taught that wisdom comes from concentration of mind. We can develop this steadiness of attention by connecting with the arising object, like the breath, and then sustaining our awareness of it. Once we develop stability of attention, instead of our struggling to keep our mind in the present, it more naturally just abides there. Although at times our attention will slip off the object, getting lost in some thought, the momentum of awareness and concentration has reached the point where the attention spontaneously rebounds to a place of mindfulness and calm abiding. That becomes the place where we reside.

With the power of concentration as the foundation, we then begin to observe the mind and body from a range of different perspectives, different stages of experience. We go through periods of tremendous happiness and clarity, of real brilliance of consciousness, of seeing things with extraordinary luminosity. These periods do not last. We then go through stages of opening to deeper and deeper understandings of suffering. Opening to that side of the Dharma is not theoretical. Our understanding of suffering comes from feeling it directly in our own life and practice.

So we have the experience of tremendous joy and luminosity. And we also have the experience of great suffering. Then we come to a place of profound equanimity. Having been through both of those other stages, our mind matures to a place where it is no longer moved: it does not grasp at pleasant things; it is not repelled by unpleasant things. Our mind attains deep, deep balance, like a calm, deep-flowing river. Out of this mature place of equanimity, the conditions arise that open our mind suddenly to the unconditioned, to what is beyond body and mind, to freedom.

Grace, or Help Along the Way

Moment-to-moment awareness—that is one accurate way to describe the great enterprise of becoming free. But there are other valid ways to characterize our path. In the broadest conception of the path, in the vast context of spiritual practice, we cultivate and nourish certain qualities that support and propel us forward into freedom. The Pali word *parami* refers to ten wholesome qualities in our minds and the accumulated power they bring to us: generosity, morality, renunciation, wisdom, energy, patience, truthfulness, resolve, lovingkindness, and equanimity.

The fact that we do not often find the word *grace* used by schools of Buddhism may allow us to connect with a fresh and immediate sense of the word by looking directly at our own experience. I feel that the paramis are one great influence in our experience that corresponds to the sense of grace, not as a theological doctrine or metaphysical concept but as something we can really feel and know.

The concept of parami reminds me of a line in a poem by Dylan Thomas: "The force that through the green fuse drives the flower." Parami does not come from some being outside ourselves; rather, it comes from our own gradually accumulated purity. A Buddhist understanding of reliance on a higher power would not necessarily involve reliance on some supernormal being. It is, rather, a reliance on these forces of purity in ourselves that are outside our small, constricted sense of *I,* and that constitute the source of grace in our lives.

In the long course of evolution in this lifetime and perhaps over many lifetimes, we have generated a power of purity in our mind by acts of generosity and lovingkindness, by deepening understanding and wisdom. This power becomes the karmic force that brings blessings in our life. So our own inner development, not an external agent, brings us this grace. Develop and strengthen the paramis within you, and from that source enjoy the blessings that result.

A poem by Galway Kinnell beautifully expresses the grace of blessings from within:

What Is the Path?

Saint Francis and the Sow

The bud
stands for all things,
even for those things that don't flower,
for everything flowers, from within, of self-blessing;
though sometimes it is necessary
to reteach a thing its loveliness,
to put a hand on the brow
of the flower
and retell it in words and in touch
it is lovely
until it flowers again from within, of self-blessing;
as Saint Francis
put his hand on the creased forehead
of the sow, and told her in words and in touch
blessings of earth on the sow, and the sow
began remembering all down her thick length,
from the earthen snout all the way
through the fodder and slops to the spiritual curl of the tail,
from the hard spininess spiked out from the spine
down through the great broken heart
to the sheer blue milken dreaminess spurting and shuddering
from the fourteen teats into the fourteen mouths sucking and
        blowing beneath them:
the long, perfect loveliness of sow.

Freedom cannot be found within the contraction of ego identification. The practice of Buddhadharma awakens us to an underlying
reality beyond that identification. As the paramis develop through
our practice—and they have been developing over lifetimes—we
experience an emergence of something called *dhammoja* in Pali, the
essence of Dharma. In deepening meditation practice we drop out
of the conceptual realm into an energy flow of awareness. Dhammoja is this energy that keeps pushing us to liberation. It is something greater than our limited sense of self.

I had a strong experience of dhammoja during one of my periods
of practice in Burma. I had been in Asia for several months and was
rapidly losing weight and physical strength. At one point my body
became so weak that I would actually topple over from my sitting
position. But even in this very weakened bodily condition, the en-

ergy from the inner flow of awareness remained so strong that the meditation continued to unfold. It was as if nothing could stop the onward-leading momentum. This experience reminded me of those stories of the Buddha visiting people who were sick or dying. He would often say to them, "Though your body is weak and full of pain, train your mind to stay alert and mindful." A taste of dhammoja shows us that we can actually do what the Buddha advised.

Another understanding of grace comes from the Buddhist worldview that recognizes beings on other planes of existence. In traditional Buddhist cultures people believe that *devas,* or celestial beings from higher planes, can work to protect, guide, and help us in different situations. The Buddha taught that devas are drawn to us through the power of our virtue and lovingkindness. As we cultivate and purify our own morality and love, we open ourselves to receive their positive energy and beneficent help.

You may or may not choose to believe this aspect of Buddhist cosmology. Our freedom does not depend on external things. You can come to full liberation whether or not you find devas credible. But a phrase from Coleridge might suggest a useful attitude: the willing suspension of disbelief. Can we remain open to possibilities of things we do not yet know for ourselves, with neither blind belief nor blind disbelief? Many things that today seem commonplace in our world, one hundred years ago would have been called miracles.

Although strong hidden influences, given the right conditions, can assist us, they cannot accomplish the work of spiritual practice for us. The beneficence of external beings like devas is secondary to the inwardly developed, liberating force of dhammoja and the paramis.

Reflecting on our own paramis can be a great help in practice. The force of delusion is so strong that most beings never see the possibility of coming out of suffering. The very notion that the mind can be purified of greed, hatred, and delusion never even occurs to most people. Only a vast reservoir of parami brings us to practice and creates the motivation and interest to do this difficult, ultimately liberating work. Appreciating the paramis within ourselves can be a cause for great self-respect and joy. Often, in the midst of the many ups and downs of practice, we forget just how powerful the paramis are in each one of us. They engender true grace in our lives.

The Role of a Teacher

Dharma practice takes us to the edge of what is known. Mostly in our life we create for ourself a domain of comfort, where everything is in place and we know where we stand. Often our mind builds strong defenses to maintain reassuring stability in our inner realm. But this security also limits us to the familiar, to the easily recognized. There are worlds of experience and ways of being that lie beyond the habits of our conditioning. Do we have the courage of heart and spirit to explore the unknown?

A teacher, guide, and spiritual friend can be of inestimable help on the path. Such a person can reveal what is hidden, point out the path, and inspire our highest aspirations. As we pass the boundaries of familiarity, we experience suffering and happiness in new and unexpected ways. Sometimes suffering spurs our efforts to be free; at other times, we simply become mired in patterns of suffering, unable to find our way out. Happiness can trap us even more. There are many nice resting places along the spiritual path. We begin to feel more peaceful, more in harmony, better adjusted, and more accepting. We relate better to others; our life gets easier. And we may decide to settle into this place of ease for a nice long rest.

A good teacher knows when a student is stuck, either in suffering or in a conditioned kind of happiness. Employing a variety of skillful means, the teacher uses everything as fuel for the fire of awakening. At times we need encouragement and loving support, at other times, perhaps a fierce wake-up call. I have appreciated this skill so much in U Pandita Sayadaw, my Burmese meditation teacher. No matter what glorious experience I have reported to him, he has seemed to remain unimpressed. Although at times I have felt disappointed, he has given me the gift of not settling for anything less than liberation.

Another wonderful teacher, Nyoshu Khenpo Rinpoche, pointed to the highest freedom in a different manner. I had gone to see him for an interview, telling him about various meditation experiences. He said, "The price of gold goes up and down, but the nature of gold remains the same." Many experiences come and go in meditation, but the pure nature of mind abides. Both by words and presence, a teacher helps us not to get caught in temporary appearances.

One area of difficulty that can arise in the teacher-student relationship is confusion between power and authority. In all domains of life we encounter people who have more understanding than we do about certain things. Acknowledging that difference opens us to learning from such people. It helps us keep a beginner's mind. But acknowledging someone's understanding in a particular area should not be confused with conferring power. We can welcome guidance, instruction, and inspiration without abandoning our own inner moral sense.

Problems related to power may come from both sides. Teachers may have had some genuine level of realization but may not yet be fully liberated, and so at times they may act from places of ignorance. Students may be too willing to surrender their own powers of discriminating wisdom in the name of spiritual humility. We often mistakenly assume that because someone has genuine understanding in one particular area, this mastery necessarily extends to all other areas of life. That may or may not be true.

In the Theravada tradition of Buddhism, the teacher is considered a *kalyana-mitta,* a spiritual friend. A true kalyana-mitta acts out of kindness and compassion for the suffering of beings. When we recognize a natural authority in teachers because of their wisdom, their knowledge, their compassion, and when they act from that natural authority, not from some less skillful place of power, then we can benefit immeasurably from their guidance. The relationship between teacher and student can be the greatest blessing of a student's life; it also has the potential for danger and abuse. Acknowledging both of these possibilities helps us distinguish between the two.

Roads to Fulfillment

The Buddha taught about four paths or roads to success, to fulfillment, roads that lead us onward. They are four different qualities of character, each reflecting a different strength of personality. If we can recognize which of them is our own particular strength, then we can build on that power we already have; we can do what has to be done.

Sometimes people have the idea that to practice the Dharma means to live without passion, without fire—that it means a cool and detached passivity. This is a very mistaken notion. Each of the four roads to power involves a tremendous passion, a great fire within us. For those of us in whom that passion stirs, the Dharma becomes the paramount commitment of our lives.

The first road to success that can fuel our commitment is zeal— the strong desire to do, to accomplish something. When we feel this quality, we sense that nothing can finally impede us. We feel that we will not be satisfied until we have realized our goal. Sometimes when I think of this quality, I think of the extraordinary enthusiasm and motivation of Olympic athletes, or great musicians, or anyone who has brought something to perfection. The quality of zeal, of ardency, carries them through their lives: "I'm going to do this! I'm going to accomplish this!" And they do, based on that strength of mind, that unwavering sense of purpose. So desire to do, a powerful aspiration and motivation, is one of the four roads to success.

The second road is the quality of energy. A person who has this resolute determination of heart feels *challenged* by the thought, "This undertaking requires great effort. I can do it." Such a person not only remains undaunted by the effort required but also finds inspiration in the challenge. It is the sense, "Whatever can be accomplished by effort, that I can do."

Some time ago I read a newspaper article about the death of the legendary racehorse Secretariat. The article beautifully eulogized this horse's courageous heart, describing how that courage manifested so superbly in all those races. When we act from that place of heart, putting out effort without holding anything back, we develop tremendous strength and power.

Dipa Ma, one of my teachers from India, exemplified this quality of heroic effort. There were times in her practice when she was very ill, so weak that she had to crawl up the stairs to the meditation hall to continue her meditation. Nothing daunted her. The last time I saw her before she died, Dipa Ma turned to me and said, "You know, you should sit for two days." She did not mean a two-day retreat; she meant one sitting two days long! Just sit, for two days! When she said this, I started to laugh because it seemed so beyond my capacity. She looked at me with deep compassion and said, "Don't be lazy."

Dipa Ma had an astonishing capacity for effort, and it brought her the kind of result that that strength of mind brings. People with this power, this characteristic, who have this strong ability to make effort, are not disheartened by how long it takes, how difficult it is. It takes months, it takes years, it doesn't matter—because the courage of the heart is there.

The Buddha also exemplified this quality. Before his awakening, when he was still seeking the truth just as we seek it, he made this determination: "If the end is attainable by human effort, I will not rest or relax until it is attained. Let only my skin and sinews and bones remain. Let my flesh and blood dry up. I will not stop the course of my effort until I win that which may be won by human ability, human effort, human exertion."

The third road to success is strong love for the Dharma, the love for the truth that keeps our mind continually absorbed in the practice. This love has great purity of consciousness and is extremely ardent. When you first fall in love—in the ordinary, worldly sense—your mind fills with thoughts of your beloved. Love for the Dharma has that level of intensity. It becomes a path to understanding when it fills our minds. We continually reflect on the Dharma, practice it; nothing else seems equally important. Such love for the Dharma keeps us going. It is our highest love, our highest value.

The last of the roads to success is the quality of inquiry, of investigation. Some people have a strong interest in understanding the deepest and most profound aspects of the teachings. They are not satisfied to know just the surface of things. This kind of mind contemplates the immensity of samsara—this round of rebirths—the immensity of the planes of existence, and the implications in our lives of this vastness of vision. A person with such fervent inquiry investigates and understands the potential for suffering and the possibilities for freedom. Such a person takes the deepest satisfaction in probing and investigating the profound mysteries of consciousness.

Someone endowed with *any one* of these four bases of power will undoubtedly come to liberation. We may free ourselves through the power of zeal, the great desire and motivation to follow the path; we may do it through the quality of heroic effort, an effort that cannot be stopped; we may come to awakening through our absorption in and love for the Dharma; or we may experience freedom through the power of investigation, the need to know and understand. Any one of these can be our path of fulfillment.

Our work is to recognize where our own strength lies, and to practice from that place of strength, to develop it, to cultivate it, and to make it even stronger. Our great life challenge is to do the work of awakening, to see that the path of practice lies in bringing these liberating qualities of heart and mind to each moment. The path of awakening is moment to moment; it is right here. Can we hold this vision and be complete in our attention in this moment? Can we be deeply inspired by what is true, remembering that our practice is never just for ourself? We practice for the benefit and welfare of all beings. The Buddha pointed out the four roads to success. The rest is up to us.

Two

How to Practice

Purpose, Effort, and Surrender

How can we have a goal in practice, feel inspired by a sense of purpose and direction, and yet avoid becoming caught in a tangle of straining and striving? This is a crucial question for anyone on a spiritual path.

All of the choices we make in our life involve some kind of purpose and goal. A clear sense of destination helps us choose more wisely the path that leads there. So when we know our purpose for meditation, we begin to understand the great significance of the spiritual journey; and that understanding in turn gives us the necessary inspiration and energy to travel the path.

The Buddha's teaching inspires the journey because he articulates so clearly where the path of practice leads: to deeper levels of insight and freedom, to that purity and happiness of a mind-heart free from grasping, free from hatred, and free from ignorance.

If you want to heighten your effort and energy for this immense journey of freedom, you might try a few reflections that have great power. Try reflecting on the very fleeting, momentary nature of your experience. Although we may understand this truth intellectually, it takes caring, wise attention to see and feel it deeply. Where has all your experience gone? Moment after moment it disappears. We may hold on to ideas or memories, but they too become just other passing, ephemeral experiences. Given this great and obvious truth of impermanence, what is really of value in your life? What is really worth cultivating?

This very reflection on impermanence motivated the Buddha-to-be to seek enlightenment in his own momentous quest. "Why should I," he asked while still a prince in his palace, "who am subject to old age, disease, and death, seek that which is also subject to old age, disease, and death?"

After his great awakening, the Buddha encouraged, exhorted, admonished others to feel the urgency that comes from knowing that all things pass away: "There are trees and the roots of trees," he told monks, nuns, and laypeople. "Meditate now, lest you regret it later." Trees provided convenient places to meditate in those days and in that climate.

The Buddha knew so clearly just how fast our life goes by, and how rare and precious a gift is the opportunity to practice, to awaken. Unless we use the time of our life well, we can be left with gnawing remorse, a feeling of having missed something of the greatest value.

You can also reflect on what first awakened your interest in your own journey of understanding. Was it some deep experience of personal suffering? Was it compassion for the suffering of others? Was it some inner groping for meaning or purpose in your life? Sometimes we lose touch with what first inspired us. It can help us to reconnect to that initial interest and inspiration. Doing so can rekindle the fire of effort, of passion for this amazing path of waking up and becoming free.

Without that fire of effort, nothing happens. We simply live out, and act out, all the old habit patterns of our conditioning. It is extremely difficult to step outside these habits, to discern in a clear, fresh way what is actually occurring, and to make choices based on wisdom rather than on reactive conditioning.

But effort alone is not enough. Valuable as this quality is, it can also lead us astray if it is overdeveloped. We can become attached to the goal of enlightenment and become very ambitious, with a kind of spiritual competitiveness or a strong self-judgment about our progress. We can strive and strain with an excessive urgency that can become desperation. Wanting something to happen *right now* gets in the way of clear seeing. It leads to frustration, disappointment, even despair.

Recognizing (often through painful personal experience) the difficulties that come from such a striving, expecting mind, many people discard the notion of goal altogether. This also is a mistake. If we abandon a sense of goal and become attached to the idea that practice is simply becoming aware and mindful in the moment, without any sense of destination, development, or deepening realization, then we lose a source of tremendous energy and inspiration.

The critical balance we need to discover in meditation practice—and indeed in all aspects of our life—is the equipoise between effort and surrender. On the surface these two qualities seem to contradict each other. How can we make effort, be purposeful, and at the same time surrender to what is happening, to the natural unfolding of our experience? Grasping this paradox is a decisive turning point in coming to understand the whole spiritual journey.

Surrender does not mean passive resignation. Rather, it means surrender to the Dharma, to the truth of the moment's experience. Such acceptance enables us to make effort, to arouse energy, but without agitation or grasping. We have a sense of spiritual urgency, while at the same time we soften and surrender to just what is happening in this moment, and then this, and then the next.

In the early years of my meditation practice, I would cultivate this quality of surrender by reminding myself that my job on retreat was just to sit and walk, sit and walk, sit and walk—and then to let whatever happened, happen. By upholding my side of the effort in this simple way, I was then able to surrender to all the ups and downs of practice. There were times that were smooth, easy, and wonderful, and there were times that were full of pain and difficulty. I just kept sitting and walking, sitting and walking. And the Dharma continued to unfold.

This balance of effort and surrender can be understood very simply. One night I walked on a path through the woods from my home to the meditation center next door. It was quite dark. Clearly I had a definite purpose and goal in mind: to reach the building on the other side of the woods. That expectation set the direction, put me on the path, kept me going. But if I did anything more than pay careful attention to where I was placing each step in each moment, I started stumbling on the rocks and uneven ground.

Or think of climbing a mountain. You need a balance of perspectives to keep you going, to keep you interested and energetic. You need to be aware of each step you take, of the ground beneath your feet, and at the same time you need to hold a vision of the summit toward which you climb. By keeping the vision—the larger context of understanding why we are walking this great path—while at the same time paying accurate, precise attention to where we are in the moment, we find the balance and the energy to accomplish our liberation.

Training the Heart

There has been an interesting discussion over the last twenty-five hundred years about where consciousness resides. Does it reside in the brain? Does it reside in the heart?

Without trying to provide a definitive answer to that question, I think it is useful at least to know that at times in meditative experience there can be a very strong sense of consciousness emanating from the heart center—not the physical heart, but rather the psychic energy center in the middle of the chest. It may be that the energy of consciousness comes from the brain and is felt at the heart, or perhaps it starts at the heart center and is processed through the brain.

Some Asian languages resolve this issue quite naturally by using exactly the same word for both heart and mind. When we say "mind" in the Buddhist sense, we do not mean just the brain or the intellect. "Mind" in this sense means consciousness: the knowing faculty, that which knows an object, along with all of the mental and emotional feeling states associated with that knowing, states that can arise in different combinations in any particular moment. So in this meditative understanding, mind and heart are really the same thing.

What, then, is the training of the heart, the transformation of consciousness? Consciousness is simply knowing. But along with each moment of knowing, different associated mental states may arise. The teachings have a lot to say about these states—unwholesome ones like greed, hatred, fear, and delusion; and wholesome ones such as mindfulness, compassion, love, and wisdom.

We can understand the training of the heart as being what the Buddha called "the four great efforts": In our practice we make the effort to diminish the unwholesome mental states that have already arisen, and to prevent those that have not yet arisen from arising. And conversely, we make the effort to strengthen those wholesome mental states that are already developed, and to cultivate and develop the wholesome states that have not yet arisen.

This, then, is the formula for transformation. First we take a close look at this heart-mind to see what is what. Through the careful practice of looking, we develop a discriminating wisdom, so that we understand for ourselves what mental states are unskillful, that is, leading to suffering, and what states are skillful, leading to happiness. And based on our own experience, our own clear seeing, we begin to arouse these four great efforts. This is the training of the heart in which we are engaged.

Meditation Instructions

Sit comfortably, with your back straight but not stiff or tense. Gently close your eyes and feel the sensations of the breath as the air passes the nostrils or upper lip. The sensations of the in-breath appear simply and naturally. Notice how the out-breath appears. Or you might choose to feel the movement of your chest or abdomen as the breath enters and leaves your body.

Wherever you choose to follow the sensations of breathing, whether the in and out at the nostrils or the movement of the chest or abdomen, train your awareness to connect clearly with the first moment of the beginning in-breath. Then sustain the attention for the duration of just that one in-coming breath. Connect again at the beginning of the out-breath and sustain your attention till the end.

It is important not to become overly ambitious. We all have the capacity to feel one breath completely. But if we try to do more than that, if we have the idea that we are going to be mindful of our breathing for half an hour, then that is much too much. To sustain unbroken attention for that amount of time is far beyond the capacity of our mind, and so we quickly become discouraged. Connect and sustain for just one breath . . . and then one more. In this way you can work well within your capacity, and your mind will begin to concentrate simply and easily.

At times other objects will arise—physical sensations, thoughts, images, emotions. Notice how all these appearances arise and change in the open awareness of mind. Often we become distracted, lost in the display of experience, no longer mindful. As soon as you remember, come back to the simple state of awareness.

It can be helpful in the beginning to focus primarily, although not exclusively, on the breath. Focusing in this way helps stabilize attention, keeping us mindful and alert. Bringing the mind back to a primary object, like the breath, takes a certain quality of effort, and that effort builds energy. It is like doing a repetitive exercise to develop muscular strength. You keep doing it and the body gets stronger. Coming back to the primary object is mental exercise. We come back to the breath, again and again, and slowly the mind grows stronger and more stable. Our level of energy rises. Then when we open to a more choiceless awareness, we perceive things in a more refined and powerful way.

If at times you feel constriction or strain in the practice, it helps to settle back and open the field of awareness. Leave the breath for a while and simply notice, in turn, whatever arises at the six sense doors (the five physical senses and the mind): hearing, seeing, pressure, tingling, thinking. Or you can rest in an open, natural awareness, paying attention only to sounds appearing and disappearing. Widening the focus of attention in this way helps the mind come to balance and spaciousness.

You can also use the technique of mental noting to strengthen mindful awareness. The art of mental noting, as a tool of meditation, requires practice and experimentation. Labeling objects of experience as they arise supports mindfulness in many different ways.

Noting should be done very softly, like a whisper in the mind, but with enough precision and accuracy so that it connects directly with the object. For example, you might label each breath, silently saying *in, out* or *rising, falling.* In addition, you may also note every other appearance that arises in meditation. When thoughts arise, note *thinking.* If physical sensations become predominant, note *pressure, vibration, tension, tingling,* or whatever it might be. If sounds or images come into the foreground, note *hearing* or *seeing.*

The note itself can be seen as another appearance in the mind, even as it functions to keep us undistracted. Labeling, like putting a frame around a picture, helps you recognize the object more clearly and gives greater focus and precision to your observation.

Mental noting supports mindfulness in another way, by showing us when awareness is reactive and when it is truly mindful. For example, we may be aware of pain in the body, but through a filter of aversion. Without the tool of noting, we often do not recognize the aversion, which may be a subtle overlay on the pain itself. The tone of voice of the mental note reveals a lot about our minds. You sit and note, *pain, pain,* but perhaps with a gritted-teeth tone to the note; the tone makes obvious the actual state of mind. Quite amazingly, simply changing the tone of the note can often change your mind state. Noting refines the quality of mindfulness, that very particular, nonreactive awareness.

Mental labeling also strengthens the effort-energy factor in the mind. Because noting does take a special effort, some people find it difficult to do in the beginning. But effort overcomes sloth and torpor; the very effort to softly note each arising object arouses energy, which keeps the practice developing and deepening.

The skillful use of mental noting keeps us energized, accurate, and mindful. Try this technique in your next sitting, even if only for a short period of time at first. Simply note each arising appearance as you become aware of it: *rising, falling; thinking, thinking; pain, pain; rising, falling.* Frame each moment of experience with a soft mental note, and observe the difference in the quality of your attention.

Be patient in learning to use this tool of practice. Sometimes people note too loudly, and it overshadows the experience. Sometimes people try too hard, becoming tight and tense with the effort. Let the note float down on the object, like a butterfly landing on a flower, or let it float up with the object, like a bubble rising. Be light, be soft, have fun.

Experiment with the technique of noting to find the most skillful way to use it. At one time in my walking practice, as I took each step slowly and mindfully, I abbreviated all the notes to the first letter. Instead of noting *lifting, moving, placing,* I started noting *l, m, p, l, m, p.* The notes seemed to slide effortlessly along right on top of each movement of the step. Yet the purpose of the noting— to keep the mind fixed and steady for the entire duration of the step, or the breath—was served.

Investigate the technique for yourself. If at times you find that noting interferes too much, or is too slow for the rapidity of change, stop labeling for a while. See what happens. Play with the volume, play with abbreviating it. Understand that it is a tool, and learn for yourself how best to use it. Observe whether it helps keep a sustained attention or not. See for yourself how the noting functions. Be flexible, and enjoy the exploration.

Nintendo Dharma

You may have noticed how easy it is to stay present when you engage in an activity you enjoy, like playing some sport, watching a movie, reading a book, or even playing Nintendo. Why can we be so concentrated in these activities, and yet find ourselves distracted and restless when we meditate? Surprisingly, this simple question can lead us to a profound understanding of suffering and freedom.

What we call mind is the naturally pure knowing faculty—invisible, clear, and lucid. In some Tibetan texts it is called "the cognizing power of emptiness." But mind includes more than just knowing, because in each moment of experience different qualities, or mental factors, arise with it and color the knowing in various ways. For example, greed, hatred, love, mindfulness, concentration, and wisdom, among many others, are all mental factors arising and passing in different moments, each functioning in its own way.

When we engage in various activities, different mental factors are at work. In Nintendo, we need to be right there with the game or we lose. The mind needs to be steady and one-pointed, with the factor of concentration quite strong. In addition to concentration, another quality of mind plays a critical role—the mental factor of perception. Perception recognizes, names, and remembers appearances by picking out their distinguishing marks. Through the power of perception we recognize each appearing object of experience: woman, man, pine tree, Abraham Lincoln, computer, car, and innumerable others. Concentration and perception keep us present and absorbed in whatever life-game is happening.

Meditation practice is different. In order to develop insight and wisdom, we need to add the factor of mindfulness to the mental equation of concentration and perception. Mindfulness goes beyond the simple recognition of what is happening. It goes beyond keeping the mind steady. Through its strong power of observation, mindfulness uncovers the characteristic nature of experience itself.

Absorption in a movie or in Nintendo does not reveal the momentariness of phenomena. We do not see the impermanence and insubstantiality of all things and events, nor do we notice the empty nature of awareness itself. Perception and concentration arise in every moment; even when the mind gets lost in thought, we still recognize what it is we are thinking. But only mindfulness reveals *that* we are thinking. This is a critical difference. Perception by itself does not lead to insight into impermanence and selflessness, because it engages us in the content and story of what appears. Mindfulness emerges from the story and notices the moment-to-moment arising and passing of sense impressions, thoughts, and consciousness itself.

If we understand these three important factors of mind clearly—concentration, perception, and mindfulness—then their coming into balance becomes the field of freedom.

Acceptance

In teaching meditation we often advise students to develop a "soft and spacious mind." But once when I used that phrase while teaching in Australia, I found that "soft mind" meant to people there something quite different from what I had intended. So it seems important to elucidate what we mean.

We mean by "soft and spacious mind" the quality of acceptance. For example, suppose you are watching your breath in meditation and you feel a sense of struggle or tension. This feeling of struggle may be a sign that something else is happening in your experience that you are not recognizing or allowing. Perhaps you are not opening to some other sensation in the body, some discomfort, or some underlying emotion. Or perhaps you have become caught up in expectation, with too much effort or striving, wanting the experience of the moment to be different from what it actually is.

Softness means opening to what is there, relaxing into it. At such a time, try this "mantra": "It's okay. Whatever it is, it's okay. Let me feel it." That is the softening of the mind. You can open to your experience with a sense of allowing, and simply be with whatever predominates: a pain, a thought, an emotion, anything.

Softening the mind involves two steps. First, become mindfully aware of whatever is most predominant. That is the core guideline for all insight meditation. So the first step is just to see, to open.

For the second step, notice how you are relating to whatever arises. Often we can be with an arising appearance but in a reactive way. If we like it, we tend to hold on to it; we become attached. If we do not like it because it is painful in some way, we tend to contract, to push away out of fear, irritation, or annoyance. Each of these responses is the opposite of acceptance.

The easiest way to relax is to stop trying to make things different. Rather than try to create another state, simply allow space for whatever is going on. If you sit down after being busy and your mind feels agitated or chaotic, try just seeing that state for what it is and accepting it. You might frame your whole mind-body experience with the mental note, *chaos, chaos.* Instead of having an agenda to change the quality of your energy, you enjoy the use of this simple key to just open to the energy that is there. This does not mean either spacing out or being entangled in your agitated thoughts. Rather, through acceptance we settle back into natural awareness of whatever is present.

Softening the mind is not so hard to do; it is largely a matter of remembering to do it. "It's okay, let me just feel this." Then things settle down by themselves in a natural way. Struggle comes from not accepting what is present.

Often in meditative language we speak of letting go of things: let go of thoughts, let go of emotions, let go of pain. Sometimes that is not exactly the right phrase, because letting go suggests that you need to do something. A better phrase to work with is "Let it be." Let it be. Everything comes and goes by itself. We do not have to do anything to make it come, or to make it go, or to let it go. We just have to let it be.

In order to let it all be, we need to grasp a difficult but essential lesson for meditation practice, and indeed for all aspects of our life. Having pleasant feelings and avoiding unpleasant ones is not the purpose of our practice. The purpose of mindfulness practice is freedom. When we purify our mind of the afflictive emotions of greed, hatred, and delusion, we come to the end of suffering. So the important thing in meditation is not whether we experience pleasant or unpleasant feelings, but rather how we *relate* to those feelings. If we relate with mindfulness—that is, simply noticing, simply observing—then in that moment of mindfulness we are purifying our heart, because in that moment we are free from greed for the pleasant, aversion to the unpleasant, and delusion about what is really there.

The meditative journey is not about always feeling good. Many times we may feel terrible. That's fine. What we want is to open to the entire range of what this mind and body are about. Sometimes we feel wonderful and happy and inspired, and at other times we deeply feel different aspects of suffering.

It takes courage and determination to be willing to see all of these parts of ourselves. There are some dark corners in the heart that we may not have been willing to look at before, or to explore. They will surely come up. Sometimes even the buildup of energy that happens in the practice can feel like an uncomfortable stretch. Such experiences of the unsatisfactory aspects of our life are all part of what meditation is about; freedom cannot happen without them. The practice is opening, it is stretching, and most important, it is liberating.

This lesson of right understanding is a very hard transition to make. Can you let in deeply, right now, this crucial knowledge that the practice is really not about pleasant feelings? Can you begin to undo the strong conditioning in your mind that tells you that only pleasant feelings are acceptable? What happens in the meditation is something entirely different from this ancient conditioning that keeps us bound to suffering. Through meditation we open both to what is pleasant and to what is unpleasant with genuine acceptance and balance.

Years ago I rented a little house for the summer months in one of the hill stations of India. It was a cottage high in the mountains, exquisitely beautiful and very quiet. There I planned to devote four months to meditation practice.

A few weeks after I arrived, the Delhi Girls, a kind of Girl Scout group, set up camp in a clearing below the house. They hooked up loudspeakers that blasted music from six in the morning until ten or eleven at night. I could not believe it. I considered complaining to the mayor of the town, and wrote him many angry letters in my mind, but the din did not seem to bother anyone but me.

It was a great challenge to my equanimity. After going through all the struggles, all the anger, all the resentment, at a certain point my mind surrendered. There was nothing to do about the situation. With surrender, it was okay. There was the sound, the noise. It was fine. Finally, I just let it be.

Not Seeing Dukkha Is Dukkha

In order to relate well to unpleasant experience, we first must know that it is there. The nonseeing of suffering keeps us locked into the suffering. Seeing it clearly and precisely allows us to open to whatever form of suffering it is, and that opening and acceptance in turn allow the discomfort to wash through our consciousness and away.

Suppose your body is carrying a lot of discomfort or tension, but you are not aware of it; you are carrying it around without knowing it. That discomfort unconsciously conditions how you are, how you feel. When that physical discomfort becomes predominant enough, you turn your attention to it. If you can open to it with acceptance, what follows is a sense of relaxation. The combined power of clear seeing plus acceptance brings the relaxation, the relief.

The painful sensation may still be there, but now your relationship to it is quite different. You relate to it now out of the condition of peace, rather than out of delusion or not seeing. The same dynamic can happen equally with painful physical sensations and with painful emotions.

Some time ago a situation caused me intense embarrassment. Although I knew that I was experiencing a very uncomfortable state, I did not know just what I was feeling, and until I was able to identify it, there was so much suffering.

I was trying in every way I could imagine to get out of the situation causing me this pain. After suffering for some time like this, I finally said, "What is going on here?" I settled back, took a close look at my mind, and saw: "Oh, this is the feeling of embarrassment." In that moment of clear seeing and a willingness to be with it, all of the dukkha went away. *Dukkha* is the Pali word for unsatisfactoriness or suffering. I saw that embarrassment was an unpleasant feeling arising at that time out of certain conditions, and that it was okay simply to feel it. And then it left. This was much easier than trying to rearrange my life to avoid the feeling.

There is another way in which not seeing dukkha is dukkha. "Ignorance is bliss" may be one of history's all-time most popular adages. Its popular wisdom tells us that if we do not know that our action is unwholesome, it does not matter so much, that our igno-rance in some way excuses what we do. In fact, the opposite is true.

It is better to do something unskillful knowing that it is unskillful than to do it without that knowledge. From the Buddhist perspec-tive, that knowing is a seed of wisdom—a possibility of coming to understand and at some point refraining from such action. So the knowing *mitigates* the unwholesomeness of the action. If, on the other hand, we do not know that the action is unskillful, the mental state of delusion or ignorance *compounds* the unwholesomeness. The power of such ignorance is a tremendous force for suffering in the world, as we can see in the front page of any newspaper.

When we do not know the harm in our actions, we cannot dis-criminate between skillful and unskillful, which leaves us the uncon-scious slaves of habits and desires. Without the wisdom of that dis-crimination, we have no chance to make wise choices. So being aware of the dukkha in unwholesome actions is a freer state than if we are just going along enmeshed in them, identified with them, and ignorant.

All of this is to say that as you open to the different kinds of dukkha, you should remain confident—you are opening to under-standing.

Understanding Pain

In the same way that we unblock our resistance to unpleasant mental and emotional experience, we also develop the liberating gift of relating skillfully to physical pain. It is important to learn about physical pain, to learn how to open to it, because how we relate to pain in meditation is symptomatic of how we relate to all the unpleasant things in our life.

The Buddha reminded us of a great and obvious truth when he taught that being born results inevitably in growth, decay, and death. If we have a body, we can be certain that at times we will also have pain and illness, and we can know for sure that our body will die. Much of meditation practice is opening to this reality in a very immediate way—not merely thinking about it, but experiencing it directly and deeply.

When physical pain predominates in your practice, you can try different strategies of awareness. First, notice the general area of sensation—for example, the knee or back. Simply be aware of the whole area, letting your mind relax and settle into the physical sensations. Second, observe precisely the particular nature of the sensations. Are they burning, pressure, searing, tightness, piercing, twisting, or some other variant of bodily feeling? By noting the particular quality of what you feel, your mind becomes more concentrated.

After you recognize just what is actually there, the third step brings you even deeper. Send your awareness very precisely within the area of sensation to the exact pinpoint of greatest intensity. Notice what happens to that pinpoint of feeling. Usually it will change in some way, and another pinpoint will become most intense. Then move your attention to that point, and then to the next—something like "following the dots" of intensity.

When your mind becomes tired, come back to awareness of the whole area, or even back to your breath. It is usually better to go back and forth between the breath and the pain for intervals of several minutes at a time, because our mind has a tendency to wither, to pull back, to become tired when we experience long periods of intense unpleasant feeling. Unless we work skillfully with pain, it can exhaust our mind, and then mindfulness and energy decrease. Alternating between the breath and the pain keeps us more alert and energetic.

This alternation helps develop energy in another way as well. When pain is strong, the mind at first inclines to it without much mental exercise. It seldom wanders. Because we do not have to make much effort to stay with the pain, the mental quality of energy in our mind may become weaker. But if we come back to the breath at times, even when the pain is predominant, then a strong intentionality of effort develops. Periodically returning to the breath builds more and more energy. Then, when we again observe the pain, we experience it on a very different level.

This crucial buildup of momentum deepens our practice. It acts like a particle accelerator in nuclear physics; the particles go faster and faster until they are able to split atoms. In meditation practice, we build the energy of awareness until it grows powerful enough to see entirely different levels of reality.

Such increasing momentum comes from continuity of awareness and the periodic effort to return to the primary object of our meditation. *Forcing* the attention from pain back to our breath is, of course, counterproductive. But if we shepherd the mind back in a tender way, we conserve and build energy until we tap the power within us to realize deeper levels of understanding.

As we open to physical pain in meditation, we also discover so much of our conditioning about it. We see our aversion and fear; we watch the mind condemn the pain and close off to it. We all relate to pain in many unhelpful ways that are not conducive to peace in the heart. And as we continue the practice of mindful attention, it is wonderful to see a transformation begin to take place.

When I first began sitting, the pain in my knees was too excruciating to sit cross-legged for even ten minutes. I was constantly forced by discomfort to move and change positions. Then I thought, "Maybe I'll just sit in a chair." But since I am quite tall, an ordinary chair was not high enough, so I elevated my meditation chair on some bricks. Then the mosquitoes were bothering me, so I put a mosquito net over the chair. Pretty soon I had constructed this great meditation throne in order to be really comfortable! Every so often my meditation teacher, Munindra-ji, would visit me where I was sitting, and I was really embarrassed.

Although at first I clearly did not have much tolerance for pain, slowly my mind became stronger and less fearful. I learned how to relax into the pain, rather than to tense and tighten every time it arose.

The value of altering our relationship to pain goes far beyond how and where we sit. Times of discomfort teach us how to practice freedom in all those life situations that make us uncomfortable. How are we relating just now, in this moment, to discomfort, pain, not getting what we want? I find it so interesting to see, over and over again, how in those situations we think are intolerable, it is often our own resistance that *makes* them intolerable. The problem lies not in the situations but rather in our inability just to be with them, just to open to them.

But we also need to recognize our limits in certain situations. Sometimes experiences are too overwhelming to open to all at once. We may need to back off for a while, or to approach them gradually. Learning this balance is the key to so much of our practice. With how much can we just be in a soft and gentle way before we close off, before we say, "This is too much"? Extending our limits makes us strong. Through this simple practice we develop a power of mind, a great capacity to be with painful situations. That strength transforms how we live our life.

Feeling Good, Feeling Bad: Progress in Meditation

Our entrenched programming to avoid pain and to grasp at pleasure shows up in our practice in yet another major way. We too often misunderstand meditation by believing that if it feels good, we are doing well, and if it hurts, we are failing as yogis. If we have a painful sitting, the meditation is not going "right," but if the feelings are pleasant, light, soft, floating, tingling, then we are successful meditators. All of us find such conditioning very hard to drop. The source of our error is simple but tenacious: we like feeling good, and we do not like it when it hurts.

Our progress in meditation does not depend on the measure of pleasure or pain in our experience. Rather, the quality of our practice has to do with how open we are to whatever is there. As the path of insight unfolds, we go through certain stages of practice where painful feelings predominate. That is just what characterizes those stages. Pleasant, rapturous, very light, or very serene feelings predominate at other stages. These experiences arise simply because we are in those particular places of practice.

The liberating path leads through many such cycles, and the pleasantness or unpleasantness of any particular experience does not in itself determine how advanced any given stage is. We could be in a later stage of pain, in which the practice is deeper than it was in an earlier stage of bliss.

So pleasant or painful feelings do not indicate how well your practice is going. The goals we seek through practice are wisdom and compassion, not some permanent tingle. How long it takes for many of us to learn this one!

I will tell you a sad little meditation story. During a time when I was doing intensive practice for a couple of months in India, my whole body dissolved into radiant vibrations of light. Every time I sat down, as soon as I closed my eyes, this energy field of light pervaded my whole body. It was wonderful; it felt terrific. "Ah! I got it!"

After those months in India, I went back to America for a while.

When I returned to India, I fully expected my body of light to travel back with me. I began sitting intensively again, but the radiant vibrations were gone. Not only was there no longer a body of light, but my body felt like a painful mass of twisted steel. As I sat and tried to move my attention through that tight and twisted block, there was so much pressure and tension, so many unpleasant sensations.

The next two years were the most frustrating and difficult period of my practice. Why? Because I was not really being mindful. I believed I was being with the pain and unpleasantness, but actually I was not accepting them, not fully opening to things just as they were. In truth I was practicing in order to get something back—that pleasant, vibrating body of light. It took me two years finally to realize that the idea in practice is not to get anything back, no matter how wonderful it might be.

What we have experienced in the past is gone. It is dead, it is a corpse. We do not have to drag the corpse along with us. We practice to open to what is present, whatever it happens to be. It tingles. It's light. It's twisted steel. It doesn't matter. When I finally understood that truth after two years of painful struggle, my practice again began to unfold. You need not take two years to figure it out. Be watchful that you are not holding on to some past experience that you are trying to re-create. That is not correct practice; it is a sure setup for suffering. Simply be open, be soft, be mindful with whatever is presenting itself. This is the path of freedom.

Spontaneity and Practice

People sometimes pull back from Dharma practice because they fear it will ruin their passion and spontaneity. They question whether mindfulness and spontaneity are compatible, or whether one kills the other. This question is quite interesting because it points to a conventional understanding of spontaneity that I think is not really spontaneity at all.

We often have an idea that unconsidered, impromptu behavior is spontaneous, and we consider it something pure. But is it? It may be just acting as a slave to conditioning. Is it some great, noble, spontaneous, pure heart creating such actions? Occasionally it may be. But it could just as well be all the habit formations of desire, greed, anger, fear, and confusion, causing us to act without reflection. We call that spontaneous. How many times have you found yourself in the middle of doing something before you know that you have even started it? That is not spontaneity. It is mechanical behavior, like sleepwalking.

A truer spontaneity reveals itself very remarkably in the practice. That is the intrinsic spontaneity of all phenomena, of the Dharma, of the whole process of life. When we establish a certain momentum of energy, mindfulness, and concentration, we begin to experience the smooth and rapid flow of all appearances, arising and passing by themselves.

We are sitting in meditation and a thought comes. Did we invite the thought? Probably not. Sometimes we do, but more often thought just arises uninvited. Sensations arise, sounds appear. The more we settle into this process of who we are, this process of the mind and body, the greater is our appreciation for the mystery of it all.

There is an awesome grace in this true rhythm of life. Here is an incredible song of the elements singing themselves. This is a far deeper sense of spontaneity, the essence of who we are. How different it is from mechanical, conditioned behavior.

So in this sense mindfulness is actually the key to spontaneity. Mindfulness is the vehicle through which we can open to the continuous, spontaneous arising and passing of all phenomena.

Coming Home

Feeling the grace of true spontaneity is closely allied to another feeling you might watch for in your practice. That experience happens when our minds make a shift in emphasis from being aware of the *content* of experience to being aware of the *process* of experience.

The contents of our minds are all quite individual, conditioned by the particular events that comprise each person's experience. Parents might often think of their children, students of their next exam, artists of their creative vision.

Some years ago I became involved in designing and building a home. At each stage of the building process, as I drove around the area, I compulsively noticed just that part of other houses that we were currently constructing in my own house. One week I noticed only roof lines, then kinds of exteriors; other weeks I would be looking at only doors or windows. Mostly in our life we are very caught up with such individual contents and concerns of our mind: the particular thoughts and emotions that arise, the particular images and stories we have of ourselves or other people, the details of our situation.

Then a gradual change happens naturally in the course of meditation practice. As we observe each of these appearances moment after moment, as we observe carefully how they behave, we begin to notice what happens to a thought, a sensation, or an emotion. Slowly our mind begins to make a shift to an awareness of the process of change itself. From this new perspective, what specifically changes becomes much less important, because we are seeing, feeling, experiencing from the inside, deeply, the momentariness of *all* phenomena. That is the feeling of coming home: dropping out of the concept or content level into a more fundamental level of being.

This feeling of coming home brings with it a related feeling of interconnectedness, because just as the changing content is individually conditioned, so the underlying process of change is universal. When we drop into the flow of phenomena arising and passing, we know the experience of all beings. Partaking in the universal creates a sense of oneness, of interconnectedness. When we understand the process in ourselves, we understand the process in everyone.

Energy

As we deepen concentration through sustained meditation, the whole nature of our experience changes; we see reality in different ways. One of the compelling discoveries for me in meditation practice has been the ongoing experience of this mind-body as an energy system.

In the beginning of our practice, we have a strong sense of the body feeling solid, both when we sit in meditation and when we move around in our daily lives. But as practice goes on, and as concentration gives us more penetrating perception, our experience of this solidity quite naturally fades and disappears. Instead we begin to feel and know the body as an energy field, a continuous flow of sensations.

One way to understand this energy flow is to see that we experience it differently as we focus our attention on different centers in the body. If we direct our awareness to our heart center, we will feel the sensations one way. If we are focused on the sexual center, we will experience different kinds of feelings. We might also place attention on the throat, the brow, the crown of the head, or anywhere else. I was quite surprised when I realized that this is all the same energy stream, simply felt as different energetic "flavors" at different places in the body.

Besides feeling the energy system we call mind-body at different centers, we can also experience sensations of energy at different vibrational frequencies. As we practice and the concentration becomes stronger, the frequency of the flow of sensations becomes finer. It is as if we keep raising the frequency of the mind-body oscillator until the flow of sensations becomes very smooth and refined. Sometimes the sensations become so refined that they disappear, and all we remain aware of is the flow of consciousness.

As you deepen your practice, you will encounter an interesting corollary to this experience of vibrational frequency that is not immediately apparent. It is really one of the subtleties of the path. In the beginning of practice we generally have great awareness of pleasant and unpleasant feelings in the body. Sexual energy is one obvious kind of compellingly pleasurable feeling. There are many other kinds of rapturous feelings as well. But as the practice proceeds, and as the frequencies of the sensations become higher and more refined, we encounter more and more neutral feelings, rather than pleasant ones.

Oddly enough, we discover that these neutral feelings are actually more enjoyable than the happy or pleasant ones. That realization comes as a surprise, because we tend to think of neutral feelings as uninteresting. In fact, they are subtler, more refined, and as our awareness becomes subtler, we resonate with them more and more fully.

This progression of appreciating first the friskier energies and then the more neutral ones is the same experience we have in the meditative cultivation of the Four Divine Abodes: the mental states of lovingkindness, compassion, sympathetic joy, and equanimity. When we practice the first three abodes, we develop wonderful, happy feelings—often extraordinary rapture and bliss. But pervading equanimity develops neutral feelings, and we experience this state as an even deeper place of well-being.

Insight

The insights of insight meditation are intuitive, not conceptual. *Intuitive* in this sense does not mean some kind of vague feeling about something; rather, it means clearly, directly seeing and experiencing how things really are.

For example, you are sitting in meditation, watching the breath. All of a sudden your mind settles into a different space. Even if it is just for a couple of moments, you feel a deeper kind of calm and peace. Instead of struggling to be with the breath, you begin just to rest with the breath in a very calm, effortless, way.

That is an insight through direct experience into the nature of calm and tranquillity. You do not think about them or reflect on them. You know that daffodils are yellow because you have seen them. You know the nature of calm and tranquillity because you have felt them in your heart.

There are many such experiences, and many levels of each one; and each time we know them directly, it is as if we open to a new way of seeing, of being. This is insight.

But often our mind becomes so excited by each new experience that we start thinking. "Look at that. I'm so calm. This is great!" Or we start reflecting discursively on impermanence or suffering or whatever the particular insight-experience has been.

We need to take a lot of care. If we fail to note such reflections and become caught up in them instead—and Dharma reflections can become extremely compelling and interesting—they themselves become a hindrance to deepening insight. Sometimes people become obsessed with Dharma thoughts, with reflections about genuine insights they have had.

So try to differentiate clearly between true intuitive insight and thinking about it. Knowing the difference can save you trouble and delay. You do not have to worry about later finding words to communicate your insights. Our mind very rarely has a problem coming up with the words. Simply staying present with each new arising appearance allows the whole Dharma journey to unfold.

Three
Freeing the Mind

Hindrances: A Dirty Cloth

Most of us, quite possibly all of us, have at times felt overpowered by one or more of the unwholesome forces in our mind. Relating successfully with these hindrances, and feeling empowered by that success, is a major part of our practice. Here are a couple of suggestions for treating harmful mental factors in a balanced way.

The first thing you might remind yourself in times of difficulty is the fact that you have already accumulated great powers of purity and liberation in your mind. That truth may be hard to remember or to believe in the midst of some mental storm of fear, anger, intense craving, or whatever. But it *is* true; otherwise you would not be here as a human being. This precious human birth is the certain result of our own past wholesome actions.

And the fact that we have been drawn to practice, the path of awakening, indicates even stronger forces of purity within us. His Holiness Dilgo Khyentse Rinpoche, one of the great Tibetan masters of this century, wrote: "Ask yourself how many of the billions of inhabitants of this planet have any idea of how rare it is to have been born as a human being. How many of those who understand the rarity of human birth ever think of using that chance to practice the Dharma? How many of those who start, continue?" Reflecting in this way on our own interest in the Dharma generates feelings of joy and confidence.

Another thing to remember as you deepen the systematic exploration of your mind in practice is the fact that though the unwholesome qualities of consciousness *appear* to be getting stronger, in fact they are not; you are only becoming more aware of them. As practice deepens, we can feel overwhelmed by the multitude of different mental hindrances that arise. We see restlessness, laziness, anger, doubt, greed, conceit, envy, and all the rest, and it sometimes seems that our mind contains nothing but these afflictive emotions.

A traditional Buddhist analogy describes this phenomenon. If you have a cloth full of grime and dirt, no particular spot on it stands out. But as the cloth becomes cleaner, each stain becomes more obvious. In the same way, as our mind becomes clearer and more lucid in meditation practice, the hindrances show themselves more noticeably.

So keep a balanced perspective as you work with thoughts and emotions in your mind and heart. It is important to see the hindrances as they arise, and to understand that the clarity to see them comes precisely from the growing purity of your consciousness.

Relating to Thoughts

Meditation is not thinking about things.

The thinking, or discursive, level of mind pervades our lives; consciously or unconsciously we all spend much or most of our lives there. But meditation is a different process that does not involve discursive thought or reflection. Because meditation is not thought, through the continuous process of silent observation, new kinds of understanding emerge.

For the purpose of meditation, nothing is particularly worth thinking about: not our childhood, not our relationships, not the great novel we always wanted to write. This does not mean that such thoughts will not come. In fact, they may come with tremendous frequency. We do not need to fight with them or struggle against them or judge them. Rather, we can simply choose not to follow the thoughts once we are aware that they have arisen. The quicker we notice that we are thinking, the quicker we can see thought's empty nature.

Our thoughts are often seductive, and meditation may pass quickly when we sit and daydream; before we know it, the hour has passed. It may have been quite an enjoyable sitting, but it was not meditation. We need to be aware of this sidetrack in practice and remember that the kind of wisdom we want to develop comes intuitively and spontaneously from silent awareness.

Although meditation is not thinking, nevertheless it can be *clear awareness of thinking.* Thought can be a very useful object of meditation. We can turn the great power of observation onto thought itself in order to learn about its inherent nature, becoming aware of its process instead of getting lost in its content.

In Dharma teaching we speak frequently about the powerful impact of identifying with phenomena. Identification imprisons us in the content of our conditioning. One of the easiest ways to understand this imprisonment is to observe the difference between being lost in thought and being mindful of it.

When we lose ourselves in thought, identification is strong. Thought sweeps up our mind and carries it away, and in a very short time we can be carried far indeed. We hop a train of association, not knowing that we have hopped on, and certainly not knowing the destination. Somewhere down the line we may wake up and realize that we have been thinking, that we have been taken for a ride. And when we step down from the train, it may be in a very different mental environment from where we jumped aboard. When we do not know that we are thinking, our thoughts carry us into so many different worlds.

What are thoughts? What is this phenomenon that so powerfully conditions our lives when we remain unaware of it, yet dissolves so completely as soon as we pay attention? What is our proper relationship to that endless display of thoughts parading through our mind?

Take a few moments right now to look directly at the thoughts arising in your mind. As an exercise, you might close your eyes and imagine yourself sitting in a movie theater watching an empty screen. Simply wait for thoughts to arise. Because you are not doing anything except waiting for thoughts to appear, you may become aware of them very quickly. What exactly are they? What happens to them? Thoughts are like magic displays that seem real when we are lost in them, but then vanish upon inspection.

But what about the strong thoughts that affect us? In meditation we are watching, watching, watching, and then all of a sudden— *whoosh!*—gone, we are lost in that one. What is that about? What are the mind states or the particular kinds of thoughts that catch us again and again, so that we forget that they are just empty phenomena passing on?

The Buddha said that we are shaped, created, and led by our thoughts. If he was right, then it is important for us to watch our thought process closely to see where we get hooked, where we are seduced through identification into creating something that brings us unhappiness. It is amazing to observe how much power we give unknowingly to uninvited thoughts: "Do this, say that, remember, plan, obsess, judge." They can drive us quite crazy, and they often do!

The kinds of thoughts we have, and the impact they have on our destiny, depend on our understanding of things. If we are in the clear, powerful space of just seeing thoughts arising and passing, then it does not matter what species of thinking appears in the mind; they are all essentially empty of any substance at all, and we can see them for the passing show that they are. These all-powerful movers and shakers of the world that create us and lead us become little energy blips in our mind, with hardly enough power to create even a ripple. They seem like transparent dewdrops evaporating in the sun.

But there are many times when we are not simply watching thoughts come and go, either because we are lost in them or because we choose to think something through, perhaps as a precursor to action. In both these cases it is crucial for us to discern wholesome from unwholesome thoughts in order to know which to give our energy to, because these thoughts do have a karmic impact; they lead us. From thoughts come actions. From actions come all sorts of consequences. Which thoughts will we invest in? Our great task is to see them clearly, so that we can choose which to act on and which simply to let be.

It takes a lot of alertness to stay aware of thoughts. They are extremely slippery. If you watch them in one place, they sneak in from another. But as practice evolves, two liberating things happen. First, our mind actually becomes quieter. Instead of being a rushing torrent, thoughts come less frequently and we enjoy an increasing sense of calm and inner peace. Second, our observing power becomes quicker and stronger. We can see thoughts much more clearly and are taken for fewer unconscious rides. Without identifying with thoughts and giving them power, our mind abides in the natural state of ease, simplicity, and peace.

Views and Opinions

Once we begin watching our thoughts closely, we notice a strong propensity to identify with a particular class of thinking, namely, views and opinions. It is useful to discriminate between having views and opinions and being attached to them. When people first recognize that strong attachment to views can create separation, division, and conflict, they sometimes conclude that we should not have views and opinions at all. But this can lead us into a difficult bind, since eliminating them proves to be quite impossible.

The task of freeing the mind involves not identifying so strongly with the particular opinions we hold. How can we do this? To see how you identify with views, try paying careful attention to your feeling states as you proceed through the day. As you go along, you may be thinking of various things when all of a sudden some opinion arises about a person or situation.

If you identify with that opinion instead of seeing it simply as it is, as an arising thought in your mind, then watch for a noticeable tightening of your mind around it, a charge, a sense of being right — those things that contract us into a space of small mind and separation.

If we pay attention to when that tightening takes place, when that charge in the mind begins to happen, then the contraction becomes a signal that we have gone from the place of having an opinion to a place of attachment to it. We are using the radar of mindfulness to pick up times of suffering, of unease, of constriction.

Like any practice, this psychic early-warning system gets better the more you use it. Things may be going along very smoothly, and then, presto, you pick up a certain glitch on the screen. You feel in your mind and body a sense of solidifying around something. That moment of feeling the glitch is the place to stop. Right here in consciousness at this moment is a precious gift: a signal telling you something is happening; you are getting caught.

If we can unhook from our attachment to views and opinions, we can then be freer in having them. We can consider more dispassionately the whole of any given situation. We can receive more respectfully other points of view, which, in turn, creates a situation of greater openness and communication.

In this way, liberation is not always dramatic fireworks. It can be the step-by-step, moment-by-moment freeing of our mind.

Judgment 500

Views and opinions held strongly enough become judgments, another prevalent pattern of conditioning we experience. We judge ourselves, we judge others, we hardly let an experience go by without judging it. Although this class of thoughts may go unnoticed in the busyness of our lives, it becomes quickly obvious as soon as we begin to watch our mind in meditation. Sometimes it feels as if our mind does little else but judge.

Probably you are plagued by recurring judgments like everyone else. If so, you may find it helpful to remember that our emphasis in Dharma practice is less on changing the pattern than on changing our relationship to it. Here are three techniques for changing your relationship to the judging mind. A couple of them are home grown; I do not think you will find them in any Buddhist texts. They came to me as I grappled with a "judgment attack" in my own practice.

I experienced this discomforting pattern of judging thoughts very clearly once when I was doing intensive meditation practice in a retreat. I found myself sitting in a place in the dining room of our meditation center where I could watch everyone come in and take food. Although I was ostensibly being mindful of eating, out of not-quite-the-corner of my eye I saw everything that was going on. I was quite amazed to see how my mind had a judgment about every single person who came in.

I did not like either how people walked (not quite mindful enough), or how much food they took, or how they were eating, or what they were wearing. It became quite disconcerting to watch that overflow of judgments in my mind. Does this sound at all familiar?

I reacted to this new awareness by becoming quite upset, first condemning all these judgments as "bad" thoughts, and then judging myself as bad for having them. Over some time it became clear to me that judging the judging was not helping at all.

The first skillful method for dealing with judgment is the old, tried-and-true, traditional method of clear mindfulness. I made an effort to notice specifically how the pattern was manifesting, noting the cascade of judging thoughts with clear awareness. By cultivating mindfulness in this way, I experienced less identification with the thoughts.

But extraordinary circumstances sometimes call for extraordinary measures, so I also evolved two other, less orthodox ways of working with the judgments. First I started counting the judgments as they arose. Every time a judging thought came into my mind, I would count: "Judging one, judging two, judging three . . . judging five hundred." At a certain point I started to laugh. I began to see these "bad" thoughts in a much lighter way, not particularly believing them and not reacting against them. A judgment arises, we can see it, we smile, and we let it go. What a breath of fresh air for the mind!

The second technique I used when these thoughts proliferated was to tack on to the end of each judgment the phrase "the sky is blue." "That person takes too much food—the sky is blue." "I don't like how they are moving—the sky is blue." "The sky is blue" is a neutral thought that can just come and go without any reaction in the mind. By adding it to the end of every judgment, I got a sense of what it would be like to let the judgment go through my mind in just the same way "the sky is blue" goes through.

So instead of fighting or struggling with judgments or other very repetitive thought patterns, instead of trying to make them stop coming, we can learn how not to react, how not to be bothered by them, and even how to smile. Try it with one of your own most bothersome patterns. "Self-hatred one, self-hatred two . . . self-hatred five hundred ninety-five . . . self-hatred ten thousand." At a certain point you are going to start smiling. You are!

And that smile will signal a very important transformation in how you relate to your stuff. The stuff is empty; it does not belong to anybody; it is not rooted in self. What feeds it is our relationship to it. We do not like it, and precisely because we do not like it, it keeps coming back. At a certain point we stop not liking it. Then it is no problem.

I have watched some of the most appalling scenarios in my mind. Okay, there they are, arising and passing. If we relate to them in a nonreactive, nonidentified way, their content does not matter. Tremendous freedom comes when we realize that from the perspective of mindful awareness the content is irrelevant.

Conceit and the Comparing Mind

Another valuable way to work with thoughts is to give close attention to conceit. In Buddhist psychology "conceit" has a special meaning: that activity of the mind that compares itself with others. When we think about ourselves as better than, equal to, or worse than someone else, we are giving expression to conceit. This comparing mind is called conceit because all forms of it—whether it is "I'm better than" or "I'm worse than," or "I'm just the same as"—come from the hallucination that there is a self; they all refer back to a feeling of self, of "I am."

There is both bad news and goods news about conceit. In fact, it is all the same news, namely, that conceit is not uprooted until the final stage of enlightenment. Even after we have realized the truth that experience is essentially selfless, that there is no "I," no self to whom experience belongs, still the habit of this comparing mind persists. We understand that the conceit itself is not "I," but still it plays itself out until we are fully liberated. So the bad news is that this comparing mind is likely to be around for a long time.

The good news is that we do not need to be discouraged or self-judgmental about conceit when it occurs. Since this pattern will be around for a while in our mind, we might as well make friends with it. When comparing thought arises, we can just see it—"Oh, here it is again"—without being surprised. We begin to work with it in an accepting way.

The antidote to conceit is to drop right back into mindfulness and to focus on the momentariness of phenomena. When our mind is caught in comparison, it is caught in a perception of self and somebody else. We enmesh ourselves in that hallucinatory, conceptual framework of self and other. We make such comparisons when we do not see how everything, including the very thought of self and other, is ceaselessly arising and passing away. The contents of these thoughts trap us because we fail to see the impermanence of the thoughts themselves. Comparing mind disappears when we succeed in seeing it.

I recall one bout I had with this comparing mind during the first retreat I did with my teacher from Burma, U Pandita Sayadaw. It was his first visit to the United States, and he ran a very demanding and rigorous retreat. We were all a little nervous, not knowing much about this monk from Asia and wanting to apply ourselves as much as possible. We were working quite hard in a demanding situation.

After some weeks I saw a few people writing in little notebooks, and each successive day someone else would begin using one. This practice was very unusual for a vipassana retreat, because people are asked not to read or write during intensive practice. And because the retreat was silent, I could not ask why they were doing it.

My mind started thinking, "U Pandita must be asking people to do something. I wonder when he's going to ask me." Soon I began noticing that the people using the notebooks were the ones I considered the really good meditators. Day after day I went for my interview with U Pandita, and he did not say anything to me about notebooks or about doing any unusual meditation assignment. I started feeling worse and worse about myself and my practice; it must be that I was not one of the "good ones."

After a while, everybody else started writing in notebooks, even the people who I thought were not such good meditators. So then I had the thought, "Well, I must be doing so well in my practice that I don't need a notebook."

Back and forth my mind went between these two views—good yogi, bad yogi, what kind of yogi?—slowly driving me a little crazy. At the end of the retreat I found out that U Pandita never asked anybody to keep a notebook! People were doing it just as a way of remembering and being able to report their experience accurately.

So it is very helpful to begin to recognize this comparing mind, this conceit of "I'm better than" or "I'm worse than" someone else. When we do not see it clearly, it becomes the source of much suffering. It makes us feel separated and apart from others; we reinforce the contraction of self.

When we stay mindful of these comparing thoughts and feelings, then we can be with them in a friendly way, without getting caught, without identifying with them. The conceit then simply becomes other empty, ephemeral thoughts, which we neither condemn nor believe as they pass through like leaves blowing in the wind. The mind stays free.

Liberating Emotions

Developing a liberated relationship to thought in all its permutations—such as opinions, judgments, and comparing—is a vital and challenging aspect of our practice. Another great challenge, perhaps greater, is learning to dance skillfully with our emotional life.

Of all the many areas of our experience, both in meditation practice and in the rest of our lives, emotions are often the most difficult to understand and to be with in a free way. Two factors contribute to this difficulty. First, emotions as appearances in the mind are amorphous; they have no clear boundaries, no definite sense of beginnings and endings. They are not as tangible as sensations nor as clearly defined as thoughts. Even when we feel them strongly, we may not be able to distinguish among them clearly.

The second obstruction to our understanding of emotions is the fact that we are deeply conditioned to identify with them. When you are in the midst of some powerful feeling such as love or anger, excitement or sadness, notice that strong sense of self, of "I," that usually comes with it. We can learn relatively easily to see the passing, impersonal nature of bodily sensations, and even thoughts, which come and go so quickly. But how much harder it is to see the impersonal or nonpersonal nature of emotions. Indeed, to many people the notion of nonpersonal emotions may even seem an oxymoron, a contradiction in terms. Emotions are often seen to be the most personal aspect of our experience.

Is there another way of understanding the rich, complex, and varied terrain of our emotional world? There are three steps in working with emotions that might lead us to a new experience of them.

The first step is taking care to recognize precisely each emotion as it arises and to learn to distinguish among subtle differences. At one time in my practice I went through a period of feeling strong sadness. It seemed to go on for days. I observed the emotion mindfully, noting *sadness, sadness,* but something about the experience felt quite stuck.

After some time I began to look at this feeling more carefully, to observe it more closely. I discovered that it was not sadness at all; it was the feeling of unhappiness. These two emotions seem close in nature, but actually they are quite different when you observe them precisely. As soon as I was able to recognize what was *actually* happening, the wave of feeling began to pass through. Until we see each emotion for what it is, we cannot come to full acceptance of it, and so we stay slightly out of alignment with what is happening and perhaps end up feeling stuck.

There are other times when emotions are so unpleasant, so uncomfortable, that we do not allow ourselves to acknowledge them at all. Instead we seek ways, consciously or unconsciously, to avoid feeling them. This pattern of denial can happen with feelings of fear, shame, anxiety, loneliness, rage, boredom, embarrassment, and many others. We find ourselves trying in every way imaginable to change the situation rather than simply to be with the feeling.

How much, and what kinds of things, do we do in our lives just so that we do not have to feel bored or lonely or afraid? Not opening to the range of emotions, not understanding that they will arise and pass away by themselves, compels us to actions that may not actually bring us happiness, but may rather keep us continually on the run. Many destructive addictions might be prevented by practicing the willingness simply to feel the unpleasantness of painful emotions. Recognizing and acknowledging emotions as they arise, particularly the difficult ones, allows us to open to them so that we can experience what the old Taoists called the ten thousand joys and the ten thousand sorrows.

Another aspect of recognizing emotions is seeing that often they come in clusters or constellations. We may be aware of the most predominant feeling, yet we may miss the feelings that are underneath it and feeding it like underground springs. For example, we may feel strong anger and be quite mindful of it but may not catch a certain self-righteousness that goes along with it. As long as we remain unaware of such associated states, the emotional fellow travelers, we may stay stuck in a painful emotion for quite a long time.

Clear recognition and acceptance of different emotions that arise in our experience lead us to the second important step in working with strong feelings. Our Western culture does not much value this method, although it is one of the foundations for happiness in our lives. I am referring to the ability to discriminate wisely between wholesome and unwholesome emotions or states of mind. The measure for making this distinction is simple: does this mind state or emotion create suffering for ourselves or others, or does it create happiness and peace?

Some states of mind are very obviously either skillful or unskillful. *Skillful,* in the Buddhist sense, refers to that which leads to happiness, to freedom, and *unskillful* to that which leads to suffering. Few would disagree that greed or hatred or ignorance are undesirable states, or that generosity, love, compassion, and understanding are worthy ones. Sometimes, though, the distinctions are subtle, difficult to make, especially when unwholesome emotions or states of mind masquerade as wholesome ones. We might mistake sorrow or grief or even outrage for a feeling of compassion. Or we might confuse the feeling of indifference with that of equanimity. They look alike, but they are really quite different, with different consequences.

So often in our society we hear and read that we need to honor our emotions, which is certainly true in the sense of recognizing, accepting, and opening to them. But that by itself is not enough. We also need to take the next step, to investigate whether a particular mind state is skillful or not. Is it bringing happiness and freedom, or is it bringing more suffering? Do we want to cultivate it, or to let it go? We always have this choice, although we often fail to exercise it.

This quality of wise discrimination can empower us tremendously. We can rarely control what emotions come into our mind and heart. But once they are there, we can acquire the freedom to relate to them in different ways. If we are unaware either of what emotion is present or of whether it is wholesome or unwholesome, then we simply act out all our old patterns of conditioning. This may keep us entangled in suffering even as we are wanting happiness. When we are aware of both of these aspects, we create the possibility for wise choice and inner freedom.

The third step in working with emotions is both the most difficult and the most liberating. That step is learning, even as we open to the whole range of feelings, not to identify with them. Identifying with the emotion—that sense of its being self, being "I"—is extra. Notice the feeling of contraction when you identify strongly with various mind states we all experience: "I'm angry," "I'm sad," "I'm happy," "I'm anxious." These moments of identification are a habituated add-on, a convention that causes a lot of heartache and pain.

From a meditative perspective, various mind states, including emotions, arise and pass away empty of any substantial nature. They come into being when certain conditions come together and disappear when the conditions change. None of them belong to anyone; they are not happening *to* anyone.

In a very real sense each mind state or emotion is expressing itself; it is desire that desires, fear that fears, love that loves. It is not you or I. Can you feel the difference between the experience of "I am angry" and the experience of "This is anger"? Through that little distinction flows a whole world of freedom. Of course, it is extremely important not to use the idea of selflessness as a vehicle for denial. True selflessness comes from openness and acceptance.

As one Tibetan Buddhist text expresses it, mind states or emotions are like clouds in the sky, without roots, without home. Identifying with an emotion as being self is like trying to tether a cloud. Can we learn to liberate all emotions, all phenomena, letting them pass through the open sky of the heart and mind?

Emotional Bondage, Emotional Freedom

"Well," you might ask, "I see the value of not identifying with emotions, not making them 'I,' but how do I actually *do* it?"

Doing it is not easy. It is so easy to get caught in emotions, lost in their energy, lost in thoughts about them. Through the entanglement of identification we create a strong sense of self, of "I": "I'm so angry!" "I'm so sad!" or happy, or whatever.

Our great challenge and potential is to learn how to stay open to the whole range of feeling, without adding this extra sense of I and mine in the midst of it. One practical device that often helps is to see three things going on in the midst of strong emotion.

When we become angry, for example, first there is some external situation prompting the anger to arise. Someone is doing or saying something we do not like, or we feel is harmful to ourself or others. Second, there is our reaction to that situation, namely, the feeling of anger. And the third component is the relationship of our mind to the anger itself.

Usually we are lost in the first two: the external situation and our reaction to it. Something happens, we get angry. As we get angry, we start thinking about what happened. All those thoughts create more anger, which in turn creates more thoughts about the situation, often with blame, self-righteousness, and hurt feelings. Thus we quickly become caught in a destructive loop.

If you seek a way out of such cycles, try turning your attention away from the situation and your reaction to it and toward the third component, the relationship of your mind to the emotion, whether it is anger, fear, or whatever. For example, in the midst of the whirlwind of anger, you might ask yourself, "How am I getting caught in this anger? How am I getting hooked by it? How am I identifying with it?"

Asking some form of that question is completely different from considering the external situation. At such a time, we are no longer sending out threads of blame that bind us to the situation, to the reaction, and to our identification with the emotion. We are no longer thinking about the external causes of the anger, so we are no longer feeding it.

We also do not ask the question for the purpose of getting an answer or having an intellectual response. Rather, the question's purpose is to help us change perspective, to take responsibility for what arises in our mind. In the moment of asking "How am I getting hooked?" we have already moved outside the anger and are looking at the way we are relating to it. It is possible in that moment for the whole mass of anger to dissolve, *without* our denying it, repressing it, or shoving it away.

Once at our meditation center in Barre, Massachusetts, I became very angry at someone for doing something I felt was quite harmful. The anger was very intense, and I was noting, *Anger, anger, anger.* My whole body was vibrating. It went on for many hours. Every time I thought about the situation, the anger became stronger.

I went to sleep feeling this way, and the intensity of that emotion and its effects on my body woke me early in the morning. It was so startling to awaken to the same level of intense angry energy that I began to ask myself, "What's happening here? How am I getting so hooked into this feeling?" At that point I was not asking these questions mechanically; I really wanted to see what was going on, why my mind was so caught, so identified with the anger.

In the very moment of asking these questions, of shifting my perspective, my whole body became softer, and the anger disappeared. It was like magic. Later that day I talked to the person at whom I had felt so angry. We were able to communicate about the problem in an easy and productive way, because the anger and blame were no longer there. So it is not that we avoid dealing with the external situation. Rather, if we can become clear in our own minds and hearts first, then the resolution can come more easily.

Probably you will not perfect this simple way to disidentify with painful emotions the first time you try it. Like any practice, we need to hone it through interest and repetition. But each time we cut through the chains of our identification, we experience a great freedom. The mind again becomes spacious and accepting. Next time you are caught up in a strong, painful emotional state, try asking yourself these three things: "What is the external situation?" "What is my reaction to it, the emotion I am feeling?" "What is my relationship to this emotion? How am I getting hooked?"

Step by step, situation by situation, we learn how it feels to be free.

Use Your Umbrella

There are different ways of dealing with experiences of overwhelming emotion when we do not have the time or space to observe and investigate. Sometimes a retreat from the situation is the most skillful response. We back off, cool out a little, and then, if the situation persists, go back and try to communicate with the person or people with whom we experience trouble.

It is also useful to realize that many things are out of our control. One of my teachers told me something very early on in my practice that has been tremendously helpful ever since; it has saved me a lot of suffering. He said, "You can't take charge of other people's minds. You can take charge of your own mind." Although we can try to communicate clearly and skillfully with other people, feel compassion for their suffering, and work to alleviate it, still, in the end, we cannot control their actions or reactions. When we understand this fact, it becomes a little easier to let go. As the quality of equanimity grows in our mind, then we are more able to be with unpleasant or disagreeable situations without our own mind becoming agitated. We learn to respond rather than react.

And there are some circumstances that do call for a forceful response. We do not always have to be passive and accepting in every predicament. Sometimes we might have to use our umbrella!

Sharon Salzberg, a friend and teaching colleague, had a frightening experience years ago, when we were both first practicing meditation in India. She and another friend had been in Calcutta with one of our teachers, Dipa Ma. When they left her, they hired a rickshaw to go to the train station. As they took a shortcut through a dark back alley, a man leaped at them violently and started to pull Sharon out of the rickshaw. It was a very scary moment. Sharon's friend finally managed to push the attacker away, and they escaped to the station unharmed.

When they arrived back in Bodh Gaya, where we were all staying, Sharon told our teacher, Munindra-ji, what had happened. He listened carefully to all the details. At the end of the story Munindra-ji said, "Oh, dear. With all the lovingkindness in your heart, you should have taken your umbrella and hit that man over the head."

Sometimes that is what we need to do. It would be easy enough to hit the man over the head with the umbrella. The difficult part would be to do it with all the lovingkindness in our heart. So that is our real practice.

That quality of being firm and decisive, of using the umbrella when nothing else avails, is something we can use in meditation, too, though it must be used with care and precision. When something unskillful in the mind keeps coming back again and again, we can find that strong and decisive place in our mind, and from there take a firm position not to get caught. It is as if we take out our umbrella—our sword of wisdom—and say, "Enough" or "Not now."

This bold action in the mind is *not* about avoidance or shoving away something unpleasant because we do not want to experience it. If we do it, we must do it with the feeling of lovingkindness, not with aversion. That is where people often make a mistake; they take out their sword of anger instead of their sword of discriminating wisdom. Wisdom says, "This mind state or emotion is unskillful, unwholesome. I've seen it many times already. Now I let it go."

We always need to find the right balance in order for any skillful means to be truly skillful. Often people are so judgmental and condemning of things in themselves and others that they need most to soften, to accept, to let things be. But it is also important to explore that place of strength and resolve in the mind, the place of the warrior within us, so that we can use our growing power to cut through unskillful states in appropriate and loving ways.

Fear Itself

"The only thing we have to fear is fear itself."

Franklin Delano Roosevelt's first words as president to his beleaguered country are the ones for which he is still most remembered; they remain familiar to many of us who were born years after they were spoken. The memorable power of Roosevelt's words lies in his reminding Americans that the most formidable danger was not in the external circumstances of the Great Depression but rather in the forces at work in their own minds.

As meditators we might pursue this understanding even further. Must we fear fear itself? How much of our creative and vital power is tied up—sometimes even paralyzed—by our fear of fear, our unwillingness to feel it and know it for what it is?

It would be difficult to overestimate the potential power of fear to control our lives. This mind state has extraordinary range of expression: from mild worry to chronic anxiety to abject terror. It can contract our mind and body and cripple our will. And not only is fear a great power in itself, it also too often provides hidden motive energy to many other states that cause us pain. Behind every act of greed lies fear of deprivation. Behind hatred and aggression lies fear of harm. Behind so much delusion lies fear of knowing and feeling painful conditions.

Do you get some sense of why working skillfully with fear can be a significant liberating act? By going beyond our fear of fear, and by unmasking fear itself, we not only free ourselves from fear's own debilitating force, but we also reduce the force of many other mental conditions that depend on it as the source of much of their power.

Mindfulness practice begins to open up everything. We open our mind to memories, to emotions, to different sensations in the body. In meditation this happens in a very organic way, because we are not searching, we are not pulling or probing, we are just sitting and watching. In the safe context of a retreat and in their own time, which is the right time, things start to emerge: the fear, the fear of fear, many of those memories, thoughts, emotions, sensations we have been afraid to experience. We begin to allow ourselves to feel it all. As these things start to come up and we feel them consciously and mindfully, with a sense of softness and acceptance, less and less energy is required to hold them down. The energy in our system begins to flow in a much freer way.

And then we look around and notice that there is less fear. We have faced what we feared; we have survived it; we even feel fine. Fear cannot survive the end of avoidance and denial. It begins to lose its domain.

The practice helps in another way. Many years ago I sat a Zen *sesshin,* or meditation retreat, with Joshu Sasaki-roshi, a fierce and demanding Zen master. It was an intense sesshin for me in that it touched in me a place of deepest fear. I felt primal fear so strong that I was sometimes even afraid to move.

I worked with that fear throughout the sesshin, and although the full intensity of it abated afterward, the deep-rooted feeling of it lasted for months. I was walking around in a space of fear, and I started relating to myself as being a fearful person. I felt the fear like a knot at the core of my being, and I thought I would have to work on it for years in order to untie it.

Months later, while a colleague and I were teaching a retreat in Texas, the two of us were walking around the retreat site. I was going on and on about my fear, about everything I had to do, and about what a huge burden it was. She finally turned to me and said something that I myself have said so many times to others: "It's only a mind state." That was just the right moment for me to hear those words. Had she said them a week earlier, they might not have had the same impact. But in that exact moment, the reminder opened me to the perspective that the fear truly did not belong to anybody. It was not attached to or part of an "I" or "me." It was just a mind state. It was there, and it would go away. There was nothing I had to do about it except to let it be.

During all that time, even though I had been observing it, in some way I had not been aware that I felt an aversion toward the fear. Because of that aversion, there was also a negative identification with it. In the moment of actually realizing that fear is just a mind state, the whole thing disappeared. I do not mean that fear never came back to me again, but from that time on I saw it much more easily.

An emotion is like a cloud passing through the sky. Sometimes it is fear or anger, sometimes it is happiness or love, sometimes it is compassion. But none of them ultimately constitute a self. They are just what they are, each manifesting its own quality. With this understanding, we can cultivate the emotions that seem helpful and simply let the others be, without aversion, without suppression, without identification.

Fear, depression, despair, unworthiness—we just watch, and we feel. It could take a long time for the process to loosen. Or it could be a moment's sudden understanding: "Oh, yes, just a mind state." People have worked with these emotions very successfully, although it often takes a lot of patience.

Munindra-ji, one of my first Dharma teachers, used to say that in spiritual practice, time is not a factor. Practice cannot be measured in time, so let go of the whole notion of when and how long. The practice is a process unfolding, and it unfolds in its own time. It is like the flowers that grow in the spring. Do you pull them up to make them grow faster? I once tried to do that with carrots in my first garden when I was eight years old. It does not work.

We do not need any particular length of time for this process of lettings things be. Why not do it now?

Thank You, Boredom

Like anger and other emotions, boredom most often fools us into diverting our energies entirely to an external situation. Thus it keeps us from liberating ourselves by seeing our relationship to the emotion itself. We make a great mistake about boredom when we think that it comes because of a particular person or situation or activity.

So much of the restlessness in our meditation practice and in our daily lives derives from this fundamental misunderstanding. How often do we try to find something new to recapture our interest, something more stimulating or more exciting? And how often does that too quickly become boring and dull, so that we range off again, looking for yet another something "better"?

To realize that boredom does not come from the *object* of our attention but rather from the *quality* of our attention is truly a transforming insight. Fritz Perls, one of those who brought Gestalt therapy to America, said, "Boredom is lack of attention." Understanding this reality brings profound changes in our lives.

Then boredom becomes a tremendously useful feedback for us. It is telling us not that the situation or person or meditation object is somehow lacking, but rather that our attention at that time is halfhearted. Instead of wallowing in boredom or complaining about it, we can see it as a friend saying to us, "Pay more attention. Get closer. Listen more carefully."

The next time you feel a lack of interest, instead of simply drowning in boredom, use it as a signal to bring your attention very close. In doing that you will see how acuity of attention brings interest and energy. Marcel Marceau, the wonderful French mime, does an act in which he goes from standing to either sitting or lying down. He changes his position completely, but you never see him stir. His increments of movement are so small that you never see any movement. Now he is standing, now he is sitting. Try doing that, moving as slowly as possible, and see if you are bored. Impossible!—precisely because it demands such close attention.

When we are with people and feeling bored, can we listen a little more carefully, stepping off the train of our own inner commenting? If we are sitting in meditation and feeling uninterested, can we come in closer to the object, not with force but with gentleness and care? What is this experience we call the breath? If someone were holding your head under water, would the breath be boring? Each breath is actually sustaining our life. Can we be with it fully, just once?

When we recognize what boredom is, it becomes a great call to awaken.

Unworthiness

Traditionally we begin meditation retreats by taking refuge. This act has deep meaning. We take refuge in Buddha, in Dharma, and in Sangha—in the awakened mind, in the path to awakening, and in the community of all those on that path. People may take refuge as a ritual or kind of ceremony. It does function on that level, but it also has a much deeper and more immediate meaning for us.

To come to the end of suffering, the way out is through. Though what the Buddha called "the sure heart's release" is the certain result of our practice if we persevere, and though at times we enjoy tastes of this wonderful blessing along the way, nonetheless much of our practice involves uncovering the closed and uncomfortable places of the heart. Freedom comes from creating a mind so spacious and clear that those places of contraction begin to dissolve because we remove our resistances to them.

At times this healing, liberating process can be challenging, because those uncomfortable places *are* uncomfortable. Taking refuge in Buddha, Dharma, and Sangha draws to our aid very powerful liberating forces that help buoy us up through the inevitable times of challenge and travail. We are not on this path alone.

One of those difficult places, a corrosive, destructive power in our consciousness, affects us in the West particularly. I refer to the mind state or emotion of unworthiness, self-hatred.

How can taking refuge help us with this particularly harmful mental habit? When we are full of anxiety, self-doubt, and feelings of unworthiness, taking refuge in Buddha helps bring us back to that place in ourselves where we acknowledge our own essential Buddha-nature. Even though we may have all of these difficult emotions, by taking refuge in Buddha we take refuge both in our own potential for enlightenment and in the wisdom of the historical Buddha. And then from that deep place of refuge, we have the power to see the self-rejection and anxiety not as things inherent in our makeup but rather as passing forces in our mind.

Once, when the Dalai Lama was visiting our meditation center in Barre, Massachusetts, in a question to him someone described deep feelings of unworthiness and self-doubt. The Dalai Lama gave a beautiful response. In my experience, he always embodies and radiates an amazing amount of compassion. You palpably feel that quality coming out of him, and in that moment it was very strong. I could feel a wave of his love for this person who felt so unworthy.

The Dalai Lama said, "You are wrong, you are absolutely wrong!" It was a powerful moment, because it gently but forcefully cut through the investment we make, the identification we have with these mind states as being who we are. This wonderful teacher knew very well, just as we all know somewhere deep within us, that underneath the doubt, the anxiety, and the fear, the essential nature of our mind and heart is pure.

We may be visited by various hindrances and defilements that color our mind for some time, but they are *only* visitors; they do not own the house. No matter what we have done in the past, no matter what has been done to us, no matter what our present life and past lives have been, we all share the great potential of wisdom and compassion. Our life is the process of the Dharma unfolding, and we simply need to open ourselves to understanding it, to realizing the truth of what is really there.

It is important not to be misled by feelings like anxiety, self-doubt, and unworthiness. We do not deny them or pretend they are not there, because they *are* there, and they *do* influence our mind in a certain way. But we do not need to give them an import they do not have.

Taking refuge. As the Dalai Lama so warmly suggested once, "Rest your head in the lap of the Buddha." Settle into Buddha-nature right here, into the nature of the Dharma, into an awareness of the Sangha, those many beings who have walked the path of awakening. Refuge is a place of safety, and this understanding of our own inherent worthiness becomes a sanctuary of safety within us.

Guilt

A close colleague of unworthiness, walking hand in hand with it through our heart and mind, is guilt. This mind state or emotion often intrudes into situations where we may have done or said unskillful things that caused suffering to ourself or to others.

It is important to know that we actually have a choice about how we treat such situations. The customary response is to condemn ourselves, to have that feeling of "I'm so bad." But this state of harsh self-judgment is really a trick of the ego. The mind or the ego tricks us into solidifying a sense of self, of "I," in a negative judgment.

This sense of self is not a solid, continuous structure in the mind that we have to get rid of. We create the sense of self anew in each moment when we are not mindful, when we are identifying with whatever is happening. So in every moment of awareness, wisdom frees us from the contraction of self, because ego delusion is as discontinuous and impermanent as everything else. The wisdom of mindfulness and the delusion of selfhood cannot coexist at the same time; the one drives out the other.

As guilt arises in our mind, it is fed when we identify with it and make it "self," when we fail to notice it with awareness. So when guilt comes, make that the object of your awareness. Note it. In the moment of recognition, acceptance, and nonidentification—this is difficult, and it may take some time to master—you can see what a flimsy paper tiger this fierce mental force really is. Guilt arises, you note it, and in that moment of noting, when you no longer identify with it, it falls away.

In contrast to guilt there is another possible response to our unskillful actions. We might think of this response as wise remorse. We acknowledge and accept that we have done something unskillful, we understand its unwholesomeness, we see that it bears certain fruits, and with wisdom we let our acknowledgment be the force for restraining such actions in the future.

Thus we avoid that slippery, inverse trick of aggrandizing ego through negative stress on self. We feel wise remorse in a mental environment of forgiveness, because forgiveness recognizes the truth of change; what happened in the past does not have to happen in the future. There is no forgiveness in guilt because we have congealed the sense of self into a kind of unchanging stasis through negative self-judgment; according to guilt, "once bad, always bad."

One time when I was in retreat, guilt came up very strongly and unpleasantly about a particular thing I had done. It came so incessantly that I drew closer to it, very interested in understanding how I was so enmeshed in it: "Okay, what's going on here? What is this? What is this suffering about?" Finally I saw that the guilt I felt was really just a ruse of the ego, which had tricked me into creating a sense of "I."

Here was the work of Mara. Mara in Buddhism is the symbolic personification of ignorance and delusion—all those thoughts and impulses that try to draw us away from liberation. When the Buddha-to-be was making his last, great effort for enlightenment, it was Mara who attacked him under the Bodhi Tree and tried to break his concentration.

When I recognized that guilt is the work of Mara, I developed a new technique of practice I call wagging the finger at Mara. Just as the Buddha described in discourses how he would exclaim, "Mara, I see you," I wagged my mental finger at Mara: "I see you!" By that wag of the finger, the identification and deception disappeared, and the guilt I had been experiencing quickly dissolved.

Then arose the feeling of genuine and wise remorse. Wise remorse freed me from being stuck, mired in the sense of "I'm so bad." Through it I understood that the particular action that had gripped my memory was unskillful, that I could make the effort not to do it again, and that I could move on.

Try this wagging-the-finger meditation next time guilt visits your heart. "Oh, you should feel bad about this. You did something really bad, and you *are* really bad!" Do you accept that approach? Do you take it? Do you claim it as "I"? If you do, Mara has won. But if you see the trick and wag your finger—"Mara, I see you!"—then thoughts of guilt may come, but you do not empower them with identification.

And then there is room for more genuine feelings of remorse. You did something unskillful. You do not deny it. You open to it. You see it. You learn from it. And then with a sense of forgiveness, you understand that it was impermanent. In such a moment you may feel that crucial mental shift from a place of tight ego involvement to one of great spaciousness, and you may delight in the fact that indeed you have a choice.

Jealousy

Jealousy can be a consuming fire in the mind, a state of great suffering. The starting place for working with it, a place that many people neglect, is seeing it, recognizing it, and feeling it without condemnation or judgment. Condemning or judging only feeds it. If we condemn ourself for being jealous, we simply strengthen a feeling of not being good enough. We become even more tied up in the painful, fiery knot, and we find it very difficult to cut ourselves free.

So the first step is not to struggle with the fact that jealousy is arising, to make a space of acceptance. From that place we can then apply the interest of investigation. We ask ourselves, "What is this? What is the nature of this emotion?" By investigating the quality of this energy in the heart and mind, by feeling the sensations of it in the body, we extricate ourself from entrapment in the content level.

If you find yourself locked into the feeling of jealousy for long periods of time, it may be necessary to drop down "below" it to seek some underlying feeling. The feeling of unworthiness or the absence of *metta,* lovingkindness, for yourself may be working in tandem with jealousy. If you do not see and acknowledge these dangerous allies, if you are not mindful of them, then they will keep fueling the jealousy.

Even though it is a very fiery state, jealousy is quite workable. But in order to deal with it skillfully, you need a lot of spaciousness, a lot of acceptance. Touch it, get underneath it, and through understanding, overcome it.

Desire

We live in a world where we naturally encounter a wide assortment of appealing sense objects: sights and sounds, tastes, sensations, interesting thoughts and ideas. Desire arises from contact with these pleasing objects, and this desire can range from obsessive passion to addictive craving to a simple passing wish for something. All of these gradations of feeling are the expressions of the wanting mind.

It is important to distinguish here between the desire of wanting associated with greed and the desire of motivation, which can be joined with either wholesome or unwholesome factors. In English we use the same word for these very different mind states, whereas in Pali, the language spoken by the Buddha, different words distinguish the various meanings of desire. In Pali the word *tanha* means the desire of craving, and the word *chanda* is translated as "desire to do." For example, the Buddha before his enlightenment had a strong desire for liberation that inspired him over countless lifetimes of practice. This was chanda, the energy of motivation to accomplish something, in this case associated with faith, wisdom, and compassion.

The grasping force of tanha runs very deep in our consciousness. In fact, the Buddha said that this kind of desire or craving is the driving force of samsara, this entire round of existence, of life and death. Desire, wanting, craving, clinging are all expressions of the greed factor in the mind. We feel it as thirst for a particular object. We become entranced by the appearance and seduced by the pleasant feeling that accompanies it. At that time we cannot clearly see the true nature of phenomena, their impermanence and selflessness.

Observe carefully what happens to your mind when it becomes entranced in the forest of desire. It is like being lost in an enchanted maze, or rapt in a delusive dream world. We weave many thoughts and fantasies around the experience we either are having or want to have, and we bind ourselves in the chains of attachment.

Strong desire in our mind not only obscures clear understanding, but also fails finally to deliver the happiness it promises. We seek out different sense pleasures for the pleasant feelings they bring. But these feelings are so impermanent that we need to look continually for another and another.

How many pleasant feelings have we already enjoyed? Too many even to count. And yet we still feel as if something is lacking, something is not complete. Without understanding how or why, we stay on the treadmill, endlessly looking for yet another pleasant experience.

It is hardest to cure a disease when the medicine we take itself *causes* the disease. We scratch the itch, and the scratching only makes it worse. We try to quench our thirst by drinking salt water, and we make ourselves thirstier. This is what happens when we believe that the only way to end desires is to fulfill them.

A different and liberating insight dawns when we begin to pay careful attention to this powerful energy in our lives. First we need to make desire the very object of our attention, so that we are fully aware when it arises in our mind. In this way we are no longer simply lost in the feelings or thoughts, but instead we see clearly what is going on.

Then we can investigate what the power of renunciation means. For many people the word *renunciation* conjures up images of hermits in caves, or unbearable ascetic disciplines. Or we might consider renunciation as something that is probably good for us but definitely burdensome. It is said that Saint Augustine offered up this prayer: "Dear God, make me chaste . . . but not yet."

But it is possible to understand renunciation in a way that resonates more deeply within us. We can begin to see that addiction is the burden, and that not buying into it is the freedom. Imagine yourself watching television with endless commercials and desiring everything you see. That would be a state of tremendous suffering compared with the peace of just letting them all pass by. To let go of the commercials on TV is easy; letting go of the endless commercials in our mind is more difficult.

One of the great gifts a meditation retreat can give us is the opportunity to learn about the impermanent nature of desire—whether it is sexual desire, desire for food, the desire to see or hear something, or whatever. Because desire frequently overcomes us, we often feel that the only way to deal with it is to gratify it in some way. We may have the idea that if we do not fulfill the desire it will be with us until we do. Yet if we have enough strength of mind just to be with it, to be mindful, we see that it goes away by itself.

What happens in meditation when we choose not to act on desire? We watch it, watch it, and at a certain point, it is gone. Although the desire may be back when conditions re-form, in the moment of its leaving it is really gone.

Desire is impermanent, like everything else! This simple but hard-to-win insight is tremendously freeing, because we begin to understand that we do not necessarily have to satisfy desires every time they dangle their bait. We see that desires do not have to be fulfilled in order to be resolved. Eventually they all leave by themselves, because they too are part of the great wheel of change.

Pay special attention to the very moments of transition when desire leaves and cool *non*wanting flows into its place. Feel that sense of release, of escaping the grip of craving in the mind. Watching that experience of being filled with a very compelling and strong desire, and then seeing, knowing, and feeling what happens as it vanishes by itself, relieves us of the tremendous burden of having necessarily to do anything about it. The mind washes free with a great sense of relief and spaciousness.

As we become more familiar with this place of freedom in the mind, we are no longer compulsively driven by the force of desire to act. We can then bring love and wisdom to bear on the choices we make. Is this desire appropriate? Is it skillful? Is this the time? We can either act on it or not, and the mind stays in balance and in peace.

Learning to be adept in our relationship to desire, the driving force of this whole samsara, is not an easy task. So be patient with yourself, and persevere in the exploration.

Four
Psychology and Dharma

Ego and Self

In a sense we can see most of the Buddha's teachings as a subtle and profound psychology of freedom. They explore the mind in depth and describe how mind creates our world—our body, our actions, even our physical environment and the events that happen to us.

If the Dharma is a spiritual psychology, how does it relate to Western concepts of the mind? Treating Buddhist and Western psychology together makes a vast topic. Here I would like just to touch on a few distinctions that may be important to people interested in this interface.

One such distinction is an apparent contradiction between Buddhist and Western conceptions of "ego" and "self." The Dharma teaches that reality is egoless, absent of self, while Western psychology speaks of the need to build a strong ego structure, a healthy self. That apparent contradiction can be confusing. But this dilemma comes only from our use of language. We use the words *ego* and *self* one way in Western psychology and another way in the Buddha's teachings.

In the Western psychological sense, "ego," or "self," refers to a certain kind of balance and strength in the mind. Having a strongly developed ego in that sense is essential to our basic well-being. We have to have that balance in order to function in the world as harmonious human beings. People with an underdeveloped or misperceived sense of self cannot operate well in the world or be at peace within themselves.

The Buddha's use of the word *self* is different from this concept of balance or mental-emotional maturity. When he refers to "self," he is talking about an idea or concept we hold of an unchanging essence to whom experience is happening. So when he talks about the absence of self, or *anatta* in Pali, he means understanding that experience does not refer back to anyone—and this is the crucial, transformative understanding that grows so deep in our practice.

Insight means seeing clearly and deeply that everything in the mind and the body is a changing process, and that there is no one behind it to whom it is happening. The thought *is* the thinker; there is no thinker apart from the thought itself. It is anger that is angry and feeling that feels. Everything is just what it is, and *only* what it is. Experience does not belong to anyone. It is precisely that extra, and mistaken, process of referral back to someone, to some notion of a core being, that creates what the Buddha called ego or "I." We superimpose an idea of ego or self on top of a reality that is actually selfless, egoless.

The processes of both developing a strong ego structure and seeing the selfless nature of experience are quite complementary, although the words sound contradictory. A healthy sense of self develops through learning to see clearly and accepting all the different parts of who we are; realizing the emptiness of self comes from not adding the burden of identification with those parts.

Self-acceptance is really an aspect of mindfulness. Being mindful means we are willing to experience all emotions, thoughts, sensations, and events of life. This acceptance creates a strong foundation of confidence, because we heal the internal split by learning to be with the whole package.

But sometimes a feeling of struggle occurs in practice because something is going on—in the body, in the emotions, or in thoughts—that we cannot open to. We do not like certain emotions: anger, unworthiness, depression, despair, loneliness, boredom, or fear; we may find it difficult to accept that shadow side of ourself. When these feelings come up and we find ourself struggling, it is not because of what they are but because of our unwillingness at that time to be accepting.

The same can be said of certain physical sensations. When body sensations become too intense or painful, we close off, we resist, we pull back. When we develop mindfulness, we grow in self-acceptance in the broadest possible sense. We learn to accept the fullness of our experience, whether it is pleasant or unpleasant.

Based on this acceptance, we can then bring a very focused awareness to seeing the impermanent, momentary nature of all these parts of ourselves. We can see that all of the thoughts, feelings, emotions, and sensations are momentary, constantly in flux. We can be with them without identification and see that they do not belong to anyone, that they are simply transient phenomena, arising and passing away.

So insight into anatta, into selflessness, grows out of self-acceptance. A healthy self and an empty self are not contradictory; it just appears so because we use the same language to describe two different things. The whole path of meditation is about understanding that the self as an unchanging entity is a fiction, an illusory mental construct. But in order to realize this truth, we need the kind of balance that Western psychology means when it talks about a strong ego. Without qualities of balance and strength in the mind, it is impossible to see that there is no one, unchanging self to whom experience happens. So you can say, juggling the two distinct meanings of the word, that in order to give up the ego you first need to develop one.

Personality and Transformation

What we call personality is the habit patterns of thought, feeling, and behavior that have been conditioned throughout our lives. In my experience, both with my Dharma teachers and with students, there is no one Dharma-personality type; the practice does not make our personality a certain way. Some practitioners are very cool, some are passionate. Some are humorous and light, others are earnest and sober. You find every type of person practicing on this path. It may be good news to you or bad, but many aspects of our personality seem to be consistent throughout our practice.

A funny story from the Buddha's time illustrates this consistency. A group of monks who were arhats, fully enlightened, were walking through the woods and came to a stream. All the monks walked through the water with great decorum, except for one of them, who just hiked up his robes, took a running start, and jumped over the stream.

The other monks were upset—insofar as enlightened beings *can* be upset. They went to the Buddha to complain to him about their colleague's indecorous behavior. He was, after all, supposed to be fully enlightened, too. The Buddha smiled and said that that monk had been a monkey for five hundred previous lifetimes. Jumping over the stream just expressed his personality after all those lifetimes of conditioning.

You can see, by the way, that this story has interesting implications for a Buddhist theory of the evolution of individuals complementary to Darwin's evolution of species.

This continuity of personality behavior notwithstanding, there are also dimensions of profound change. As we deepen in practice, we start relating to our personality traits in a different way. Instead of our being so tightly bound up and identified with our identity, our personality conditioning occurs in a much more spacious field. The particular personality forms may still play themselves out, but they are taken less to be "me" or "I."

Practice brings about attunement to the subtler aspects of energy as it manifests on all levels: thought, emotion, body. We really begin to feel things in a much fuller way than when our mind is scattered and distracted. The result is a kind of passion in dispassion. Dispassion in this sense does not mean no emotion; it means that we are no longer so identified. We no longer create a strong sense of "I" in the emotions, the thoughts, the sensations of the body. It is all still happening, but it is happening in a much vaster field of awareness because it is not so constricted by the sense of self.

As practice matures and as wisdom and compassion grow, a transformation of character begins to take place within the framework of our individual personalities. Unskillful and thoughtless patterns of behavior fall away, and each of us in our own way increasingly manifests greater loving care. Through the transformative workings of the Dharma, our thought patterns, our emotions, and our behavior become far more fluid and malleable than when we live in unawareness.

Most people believe that we are the thoughts that come through our mind. I hope not, because if we are, we are in big trouble! Those thoughts coming through have clearly been conditioned by something: by different events in our childhood, our environment, our past lives, or even some occurrence that has happened two minutes before.

The quality of our character, and indeed the whole question of our freedom or bondage, hinges on what choices we make with respect to these thoughts. Here is where mindfulness gives us so much strength and freedom, because mindfulness allows us the possibility of not just acting habitually or blindly on the energy of all those uninvited thoughts. Rather, it empowers us to choose wisely.

Even if we have chosen wrongly in the past, in the moment of awakening to the possibility of mindfulness and right action, in that moment, what we could call a character shift or character change takes place.

One story from the Buddha's time illustrates just how dependent on conditions character is, and how we can come out of that conditioning through wise attention. A bright young student of the time went to study with a famous teacher, and he soon became by far the most brilliant of the teacher's students. Many of his classmates became jealous and worked to poison the teacher's mind against him.

Finally the teacher, fearing that this brilliant student would soon displace him, kicked him out, and sent him away.

This injustice must have awakened in the young man some very deep, old pattern or conditioning of hatred, anger, and violence, on which he then acted blindly. He vowed to get revenge in a particularly gruesome form, to create a garland of a thousand fingers from a thousand victims to present to his teacher. Thus he came to be known as Angulimala, which means "garland of fingers." So Angulimala proceeded along this very fierce, very violent path. He became the scourge of the kingdom.

After Angulimala had killed 999 people, his mother, who had set out to find him, came walking though the forest where he lived. He was about to kill her to complete his garland. Somehow at that moment the Buddha, who was in the vicinity, came to know what was about to happen, and through his psychic powers he appeared in front of the young man. "Well, I'll get the thousandth finger from this fellow instead," Angulimala thought, and he ran after him.

Even though the Buddha was walking very slowly, because of the Buddha's psychic powers Angulimala could not catch up, no matter how fast he ran. Finally Angulimala shouted, "Stop!" The Buddha replied, "I have stopped. It is you who have not stopped."

Just in that moment, affected by the fearlessness, the peace, and the compassion of the Buddha, Angulimala stopped running and asked what he meant. The Buddha taught him about stopping the fires of greed, hatred, and delusion. And Angulimala, touched to the core by the Buddha's presence and words, made a different choice, which transformed his character. He followed the Buddha to the monastery, became a monk, and within a short time attained full enlightenment.

So there is hope for us all.

This story points out dramatically how we have different seeds of conditioning in our mind, and how in our long evolution through lifetimes we have done so many things automatically in reaction to conditions. There are wholesome seeds, and there are unwholesome seeds. When conditions are favorable, we generally act in one way. When conditions are unfavorable, we often act in another.

It can go on so for lifetime after lifetime, until mindfulness awakens us to the possibility of actually making a choice. In that great power of mindfulness and choice lies our true character and our true strength.

Psychotherapy and Meditation

We can often confuse certain activities of mind with meditation practice. The clearer we are about the differences among various mental modes, the more effective and powerful we can make our practice.

People sometimes wonder if they might use meditation as a time to delve into old memories or traumas, to explore specific conflicts or feelings. In other words, can meditation serve as a form of psychotherapy? Psychotherapy has tremendous value, but the meditative track is something different. The two modes are not opposed and not in conflict, and, indeed, they sometimes overlap. But to the extent that we become enmeshed or entangled in the content or story line of our thoughts and emotions, we will be hindered from developing the kinds of insight that are unique to meditation.

Many different kinds of psychological understandings may arise during meditation, about such things as our parents, our childhood, the way we relate to other people. Although this level of psychological inquiry is valid and extremely important, we do not want to divert the mind to that particular area of investigation during meditation practice.

A great range of emotions appear during meditation. Interest, desire, anger, fear, sadness, depression, elation, excitement, boredom, anxiety, happiness, gratitude, love—at different times each of these and more will be felt quite strongly. The key question is, how do we relate to what is arising? Are we relating to these emotions by thinking about them or analyzing them? Or are we relating by simply feeling and observing?

The emphasis in meditation is very much on undistracted awareness: not thinking about things, not analyzing, not getting lost in the story, but just seeing the nature of what is happening in the mind. Careful, accurate observation of the moment's reality is the key to the whole process.

Because our personal stories are so fascinating and interesting, it is helpful to practice the "not now" technique of noticing during meditation practice. Whenever your mind becomes fascinated by a particular story, simply say mentally, "Not now." This method is a gentle way of acknowledging the story's presence, and even its value, and also, for the moment, putting it aside.

Besides the need to practice bare attention without becoming enmeshed in the story line of our life, there is another important reason not to use meditation as therapy. The meditative process uncovers many deep levels of emotions, different energy centers in the body, and new experiences of the momentariness of phenomena. At times it is exhilarating, at times fearful.

One of the great protections in this vast exploration is the fact that the meditative path is an organic unfolding. We are not choosing or selecting what will arise in the mind; we have no particular agenda. Instead, we experience an unlayering, an opening, and things arise naturally in their own time.

Because of this natural unfolding, we find that mindfulness is usually strong enough to deal with whatever comes up. Sometimes it might seem like a close battle, and we wonder whether our mind is going to be strong enough to go through the inevitable storms. But because we are engaged in such an organic process, where we do not force or dig or choose, these different psychological patterns arise with a kind of aptness that makes them workable. And they are rendered workable precisely by our ability simply to note them, to be with them, and to let them go, without elaboration, without fuss.

Otherwise we can become involved in a project mentality, where the mind is all set to work on a problem. That mentality can just create more of a sense of struggle, more of a sense of self, and cause us to lose the sense of the natural unfolding of this whole process. Moreover, if we force some of these powerful issues in our psyche, instead of letting them arise naturally, we may overload, overwhelm ourselves by what comes up.

It is neither helpful nor necessary to create a polarity or conflict between these two areas or levels of mind, the meditative and the psychological. The psychological domain of understanding is of great importance in our lives, and it provides a valuable complement to what we learn in meditation. And there are many techniques of psychological investigation that may serve the purpose of this understanding much better than meditation. When we are investigating our psychological patterns, then we should use the tools that are most appropriate to that work.

The purpose of disciplined meditation practice is to stabilize awareness and open to the essential nature of mind. Once we become established in our meditation, when we are really seeing the momentary arising and passing of phenomena and the nature of awareness itself, we are not dealing so explicitly with the specific content of our conditioning. Rather, we are much more attuned to the transitory, selfless nature of phenomena. So we may go quite deep in our practice and even reach levels of genuine realization.

But these moments of awakening may not solve everything. Most often we then find another whole task of integrating our new insights and awareness into all other areas of our lives, including the psychological. Despite our deep insight, we may see patterns on the content level that negatively affect our relationships, our lives, and that we might fruitfully explore in order to make life easier for ourselves and the people around us. Even deeply experienced meditators may feel the need to work productively on the psychological level.

So there can be a wonderful interplay between these two levels of mind. The more clarity and maturity we have on the psychological level, the easier it is to settle into the meditative process, simply seeing the arising and vanishing of experience, because we do not so often become stuck struggling with the contents, with emotional conflict.

Conversely, the more insight we have in the meditation process, the easier it is to go back and work on psychological content without its being so knotted. The psychological knots untie much more easily because we have seen the essential selflessness and emptiness of all things.

Some years ago I entered Jungian therapy, which involved a lot of dream analysis. As the therapy progressed, I began to explore some of the dark, shadow side of my mind and heart. Two major insights came out of that time, and while both are obvious intellectually, they are hard to embody experientially.

The first insight was that who we are is a package composed of many different qualities. I saw clearly that I have strengths and weaknesses, skillful qualities and unskillful ones. All of them make up the "Joseph" package. Each one of us is like this. The second realization was that I do not have to judge or even change or fix the conditioning. Seeing that I could accept the whole package has been tremendously freeing.

Therapy entailed looking directly at and exploring the particular content of my conditioning. But the attitude of simply accepting it was enhanced by my meditation practice. We sit, we observe, and we learn to accept what we see because we understand that whatever arises is not self. It is not "I"; it does not belong to anybody; it is just conditioning. So we do not have to be bound up with it or identified with it. We do not even have to change anything, because acceptance and awareness give us the space to make choices, to act on those things that are skillful and simply to let the other things be.

So I see psychotherapy and meditation as being quite complementary, although distinct. To value the distinction is helpful, especially on a retreat, so that we do not spend a lot of time lost in the content, however interesting it may be.

Yogi Mind

If you think that mental illness only happens "out there," to someone else, you might have another look at the life of your mind. When we watch our mind closely in meditation, we learn that what we call mental illness is only a more extreme manifestation of something that happens to us all.

Years ago I was doing a month-long retreat in my room at the Insight Meditation Society. After a week or so, I started hearing conversations coming through the heating pipes. I thought they were somehow traveling from the center's kitchen through the pipes up to my room, which was quite far away. The conversations were, I believed, about a couple, both friends of mine. I thought I was hearing that the husband had killed the wife, and that nobody wanted to tell me because they did not want to disturb my meditation practice. Day after day these conversations came up through the pipes. It got so bad that I actually went down to ask the kitchen staff what was going on: "Why isn't anybody telling me anything?" It seemed so real!

We call this delusive imbalance "yogi mind." Meditators on retreat sometimes experience so intense an identification with thoughts and feelings that they lose all perspective. Steven Smith, a teaching colleague and friend, told me another wonderful yogi-mind story. He and his wife, Michele, were teaching a meditation retreat in Australia. The room he was staying in had two doors coming from different directions. One door opened off a bigger hall where the retreatants would often do walking meditation.

One evening Michele came in to speak with Steven, and he casually asked her why she came in a different door from the one she usually used. Just at that time a retreatant had entered the adjacent walking room and overheard Steven say, "Why did you use that door?" This was at ten o'clock at night. At four in the morning the yogi went into Steven's room, woke him up, and said, "Why did you ask me which door?" All night long the retreatant's mind had been obsessing about why he should or should not have come in that door.

You can see how important it is to recognize yogi mind, both in the more obvious cases, when it happens on retreat, and in the many and more subtle examples of it in our daily lives. Whenever you cannot let go of a thought or an emotion that is inappropriate to the actual situation, and when identification with the thought is intense and obsessive, then recognizing this phenomenon as yogi mind helps you to come out of it sooner than you would otherwise. Our mind can so easily get stuck in its own projections. Understanding how we have become stuck can make the difference between mental imprisonment and mental freedom.

Such obsessive identification really is not so different from mental illness, and it can actually lead to quite severe mental disorder. When our mind identifies compulsively with particular thoughts or feelings, it becomes addicted. In those times there is no ability to disidentify with the thoughts or feelings, and so our mind is not afforded the great protection of mindfulness. We are swept up into a vortex of thoughts and emotions, with no place of rest or ease in that state.

Identification can also obstruct our communication with others. We become identified with a point of view, and that leads to anger, defensiveness, or aggression in communication. The problem is not the content of what we are saying but the sense of strong identification with the content. When there is little mindfulness and strong attachment, identification with our particular opinions creates polarity.

So it seems useful not to split mental illness off to "somewhere out there." We all feel its affliction to some degree or other, and meditation can be the tool whereby we make ourselves sane.

Five
Selflessness

Big Dipper

The most puzzling aspect of the Buddha's teaching is the idea and experience of no-self. So many questions arise: If there is no self, who makes effort in practice, who gets reborn, who has memories, who gets angry, who falls in love? What does "no-self" mean?

Often people are afraid of this idea, perhaps imagining that they will vanish into the void. But deeply understanding no-self is the great jewel of the Buddha's teaching; it is the heart of a free mind. A Sri Lankan monk once expressed it succinctly: "No self, no problem."

As mindfulness becomes stronger we begin opening to this radically transformative way of understanding ourselves and the world. We find we are not who we thought ourselves to be. We are not our body, not our thoughts, not our emotions. We discover that the whole notion of self, of "I," is a concept, a mental fabrication.

But if there really is no "I," no ego, why do most of us believe in one? Suppose we ask the man or woman on the street, "Is there an I? Is there a self?" Almost everybody will say, "Of course there is." Where does this firm, and usually unquestioned, belief come from? Our task is to understand how our mind creates this deeply conditioned idea of self, and to see how we can free ourselves from the power of this great illusion.

Mind is the faculty of cognizance, of knowing. When we look for it, we find it invisible, clear, lucid, and naturally pure. Mind knows all sense appearances and different mind objects, like thoughts and emotions. It simply knows. Imagine a corpse lying on the ground with loud sounds happening all around. The body is there, the ear is there, but no hearing takes place. Why? Because mind, the knowing faculty, is absent. Awareness itself is the most profound, everyday mystery of our lives.

Mind is also more than just knowing. In every moment various mental qualities arise with knowing and modifying it in different ways. Greed, hatred, love, mindfulness, concentration, conceit, despair, compassion are some examples of these mental factors. They each have their own flavor. Some are wholesome, bringing us happiness, others are unwholesome, bringing suffering. So, there is the natural purity and clarity of consciousness, of knowing, and a great variety of mental factors arising and passing away in different moments.

One particular factor of mind often gets out of balance and keeps us imprisoned in the conventional idea of self. This is the factor of perception, whose function is to recognize appearances by picking out their distinguishing characteristics and then to store them in memory through the use of concepts. *Woman, man, tree, car, city, ocean* are just a few examples of the innumerable things we recognize through perception.

When perception arises along with mindfulness, then the surface recognition frames the appearance for deeper and more careful observation. But when perception functions without mindfulness, then we recognize and remember only the appearance of things.

A story illustrates how limiting our familiar concepts can be. A friend's son was in the first grade of school, and his teacher asked the class, "What is the color of apples?" Most of the children answered red. A few said green. Kevin, my friend's son, raised his hand and said white. The teacher tried to explain that apples could be red, green, or sometimes golden, but never white. Kevin was quite insistent and finally said, "Look inside." Perception without mindfulness keeps us on the surface of things, and we often miss other levels of reality.

One deeply conditioned perception we have about ourself and the world is incorrect and leads us to many inaccurate conclusions. It keeps us from understanding what is true. This is the perception of the basic solidity of things. In his book *Crazy Wisdom,* Wes Nisker writes:

> Our language behaves as though reality were solid. On the simplest level, it positions a subject and an object, which we think of as real, on opposite sides of a verb, which we think of as less than real. Perhaps the Hopi language reflects more closely the laws of nature. For the Hopi, the nouns are verbs. It is inherent in the language that everything is interacting or in process.
>
> Many physicists also tell us that action is all there is. None-

theless, our language keeps piling up "static" things, leaving us stuck under the illusion of solidity.

As long as we remain stuck in this illusion, we cannot clearly see or understand the impermanent, insubstantial nature of momentary phenomena. Although we may know the truth of change intellectually, in order for it to transform our understanding we need actually to experience it in ourself.

Why do we have this perception of solidity? Why is it so deeply conditioned as our view of reality? This hallucination of perception arises from the great rapidity of changing phenomena. When we go to the movies we cannot see the separate frames of film. They move too quickly to be noticed, and so we remain in the illusion of appearances, overlooking the reality of how the magic works. Of course, in a movie theater that is the whole idea; we go specifically for the illusion. However, when we overlook the reality of our life, it has more serious and far-reaching consequences.

The perception of solidity also comes from observing things from a distance. When we look at an ordinary object like a chair or a table, it appears quite solid. Yet if we put that same object under a powerful microscope, whole new worlds emerge. When we look at trees from a distance, we just see an undifferentiated mass of color. But as we get closer, we can distinguish individual leaves, and even the small distinct parts of the leaves.

Because we usually do not observe phenomena closely, we satisfy ourself with a surface impression that does not reveal the composite nature of all phenomena. For example, what is your sense of your body? Do you relate to it as a composite of many different organs, energies, and systems, or do you view it as something solid that you name "body" and then claim as being "mine"?

When we observe the body carefully, the concept "body" disappears. We then experience it as a world of changing elements. You can make a very simple experiment to verify this fact. Just now move your index finger very slowly, carefully feeling the small sensations of the movement. It helps if you do this without looking at your hand. As you continue moving your finger up and down, concentrating on the sensations, what happens to the idea of "finger"? It disappears. When you stay in the bare awareness of your experience, the concept vanishes, and you know the actual changing sensations.

When perception is stronger than mindfulness, we recognize various appearances and create concepts such as "body," "car," "house," or "person" to describe these apparent realities. We then take these concepts to be actually existing things and begin to live in the world of concepts, losing sight of the underlying, insubstantial nature of phenomena.

In just the same way, by not examining carefully the composite nature of what we call self, we become attached to the concept and believe that it has some inherent existence. We fail to see that what we are is a constellation of rapidly changing elements. Life is a process of becoming, of conditions arising and passing; it is not happening *to* anyone. There is no being behind it to whom it happens.

On some clear night, go outside, look up at the sky, and see if you can find the Big Dipper. For most people that is a familiar constellation, easy to pick out from all the other stars. But is there really a Big Dipper up there in the sky?

There is no Big Dipper up there. "Big Dipper" is a concept. Humans looked, saw a certain pattern, and then created a concept in our collective mind to describe it. That concept is useful because it helps us recognize the constellation. But it also has another, less useful effect. By creating the concept "Big Dipper," we separate out those stars from all the rest, and then, if we become attached to the idea of that separation, we lose the sense of the night sky's wholeness, its oneness. Does the separation actually exist in the sky? No. We created it through the use of a concept.

Does anything change in the sky when we understand that there is no Big Dipper? No. The stars in the sky remain just the same, and the pattern of the stars remains the same. We simply see that the concept that names the pattern of stars, and that separates those particular ones from all the others, does not have any independent existence.

Likewise, realizing that "self" is a concept revolutionizes our understanding by revealing how things have always been. Each one of us is a constellation of mental-physical processes. We recognize the familiar pattern, name it, and then become so identified with the concept that we fall into the great illusion of believing that some being is ultimately there. "Joseph" is just the same as "Big Dipper." "Joseph" is a concept, a name given to a certain pattern of elements, just as Big Dipper is a name given to a pattern of stars.

Our practice is to awaken from the illusion of taking concepts to be the reality, so that we can live in a clear awareness of how things actually are. It should be easy to free ourself from attachment to concepts, . . . but it is not. On some clear and starry night, quietly look up at the sky and observe whether it is possible *not* to see the Big Dipper. We have a hard time not seeing it because of strong, conditioned habits of recognition.

Of course, we need concepts, and in many situations they serve us very well. We use various concepts as convenient designations, but if we understand that the words do not refer to solid "things" that have independent existence in themselves, then we stay free in the use of them. Problems only arise when we forget that they are constructs of our own mind, and impute a reality to them that they do not inherently have.

Meditation helps us see with bare attention just what is there. We may still use concepts when appropriate, but we do not lose touch with the reality behind them. We learn to look at the sky with a clear and silent mind; we learn to look at ourself with the same clarity and stillness.

Kalu Rinpoche, one of the great Tibetan meditation masters of this century, wrote:

> You live in illusion and in the appearance of things. There is a
> Reality. You are the Reality. But you do not know it. If you
> wake up to that Reality, you will know that you are nothing,
> and, being nothing, you are everything. That is all.

Birth of the Ego

While attachment to concept creates the belief in "self," another process altogether engenders the feeling of "self." Even as we begin to see the composite nature of our experience, understanding that there is no metaphysical presence we can call "I," still we have the strong habit of identifying with various elements of changing experience. And it is this process of identification that gives birth to the ego.

When we identify with thoughts that arise in our mind, when we are lost in them, captured by them, then we have the sense, "I'm thinking" or "These are my thoughts." This process of identification happens with thoughts, sensations, emotions, or images. The experiences themselves simply appear and disappear, not belonging to anyone, but the moment we identify with them, we have created a sense of self, a massive hallucination of perception.

Although we have become profoundly habituated to this delusion, through the practice of clear awareness we allow the process of knowing different experiences to unfold spontaneously. The power of mindfulness in each moment frees the mind from the contraction of identification. A thought arises; it comes and goes. It does not belong to me; it is just a phenomenon with no one behind it. If moment after moment we reside in this place of nonidentification, of emptiness of self, we reside in a place of freedom.

As awareness becomes stronger, we learn from our direct experience that every single appearance arises and passes away. In every moment, some object—a sight, a sound, a smell, a taste, a sensation, a thought—appears and is known. When we notice this level of impermanence, we begin to understand that these arising and quickly passing objects are not "I," not self, precisely because we see them disappear in the very moment of noticing. They simply do not have enough continuity to compose a "self." Conversely, through not seeing the momentariness of phenomena, through not seeing the truth of this changing nature, wrong view jumps in and says, "Yes, this experience is me, this is who I am."

Pay close attention to those times when your mind is lost in thought, creating whole dramas through the process of identification. Then notice those times when mindfulness is quite keen, and you simply see the thoughts come and go. There is quite a difference between these two inner worldviews and the contraction or spaciousness they create in our consciousness. In the moment of natural awareness, seeing the arising and passing of phenomena, there is no identification, no self.

No Parachute, No Ground

Understanding "no-self" does not come from destroying something we call "self" or "ego." The great awakening or discovery of the Buddha revealed that there was no self, no permanent I, to begin with. So if there is nothing we have to get rid of, then understanding selflessness very simply comes from careful awareness of what actually is happening moment to moment.

It does not take too long to get a beginning sense that appearances arising in consciousness are not self, because we see how they just keep coming and going. A subtle identification can still take place, however, with the knowing faculty itself: "I'm the one who's knowing all these changing objects." We might believe the knowing is I, is self. Because knowing, or consciousness, is much more subtle than other arising objects, you might find it difficult, at first, to be mindful of it. But as the mind's power of steadiness, stillness, and clarity grows stronger, we can actually become aware of awareness.

At certain stages of meditation practice, it becomes clear that consciousness itself is a changing process. This discovery can be unsettling, because for so long we have identified with the faculty of knowing as being most essentially who we are, taking it to be our soul, our self, our center. And now we see that it, too, just like all other phenomena, continuously appears and passes away.

Imagine yourself dropping out of an airplane and free-falling for the first few minutes. Imagine the sense of exhilaration. But then you realize that you do not have a parachute, so you panic as you fall through space. Falling, falling, falling, filled with terror that you do not have a parachute . . . until a certain moment arrives when you realize that there is no ground! At that point of understanding, you just enjoy the ride.

We often go through a similar emotional sequence in meditation practice. As our identification with things loosens up a little, and we see the rapidity of change, at first there can be real exhilaration, a greater sense of spaciousness. But feelings of panic can come when we realize that there is nothing at all to hold on to. Both the objects of awareness and the faculty knowing them are continuously falling away, like water over a waterfall. We understand now, on a deeper level, that nothing we grasp at for security actually provides it. But as we continue with the practice, enlightenment dawns: there is no ground to hit and no *one* to hit it—just empty phenomena rolling on. Then we feel the great relief of letting go, the deep feeling of equanimity, and the joy of ease.

Coming to Zero

The Buddha gave one very short discourse that expresses the insight of selflessness very succinctly: "Whenever you see a form, let there be just seeing; whenever you hear a sound, let there be just hearing; when you smell an odor, let there be just smelling; when you taste a flavor, let there be just tasting; when you experience a physical sensation, let there be just sensing; and when a thought arises, let it be just a natural phenomenon arising in the mind. When it is like this, there will be no self, there will be no moving about here and there, and no stopping anywhere. That is the end of dukkha, the end of suffering."

What does this pithy teaching mean? In each moment there is just the arising experience, and the sense of "I" or "self" or "me" or "mine" is something we are adding to it. When we say "my thought" or "I'm thinking," the "my" or "I" is extra; they do not belong to the thought itself.

As this understanding of no-self grows in practice, we often feel that the flow of phenomena rolls on by itself. No one is doing anything; it all just happens. We see more deeply the empty, insubstantial nature of phenomena. The beautiful appearance of a rainbow exemplifies this meaning of emptiness. We see a rainbow in the sky and often feel a moment's thrill. Yet on another level, no "thing" called rainbow really exists. It is an appearance due to certain conditions that themselves are continuously transforming. Can we live on both these levels at once, engaging in the world of appearances with the freeing wisdom of emptiness?

The moment of opening to the unconditioned, nirvana, confirms most deeply the liberating emptiness of self. In that moment we come to zero. Zero is perhaps the most powerful number: it adds nothing and transforms everything. It is no thing, and yet is not nothing. Coming to zero brings us beyond the somethingness of self.

From this understanding of selflessness comes a deep connection with everything. We need not rely on certain forms of relationship to feel connectedness, because there is no longer separation. There is no one to be separate. The writer Wei Wu Wei expressed this same insight regarding humility: "True humility is the absence of anyone to be proud." Humility is not a stance; it is simply the absence of self. In the same way, relationship is the absence of separation, and it can be felt with each breath, each sensation, each thought, each cloud in the sky, each person that we meet. "And being nothing, you are everything. That is all."

Ecstasy and Emptiness

Ecstasy can mean different things, and it can come from many different causes. In the course of meditation practice, ecstatic feelings often flood our consciousness when our mind is pure, bright, and luminous. Although they may be wonderful feelings, they arise because of certain conditions and will inevitably pass away.

There is another kind of ecstasy. It results from the wisdom of emptiness, of seeing the impermanent, insubstantial nature of all phenomena, where there is no clinging, no attachment, and no fear. In this experience, we become one with the unfolding process of life. This oneness is quite subtle, because it is the oneness of becoming zero. It is expressed quite beautifully by the Chinese poet Li Po:

> We sit together, the mountain and me,
> until only the mountain remains.

Six
Karma

The Light of the World

The unfolding of our life begins in our mind. The Buddha said, "Mind is the forerunner of all things." What is this mind out of which our life unfolds?

When we look at mind directly, we see it as dynamic, continuously changing, conditioned and reconditioned by all the different mental qualities that arise and pass away within it—qualities like love, fear, anger, joy, mindfulness, ignorance, and many more. Sometimes these qualities work harmoniously with one another, and sometimes our mind seems engaged in a Star Wars of mental factors.

Vipassana means seeing things clearly, as they are. Through meditative exploration we experience immediately and intimately which qualities of mind are the forerunners of suffering, and which ones lead to freedom. Such understanding is no longer secondhand knowledge; we comprehend directly for ourself. This means coming to see both what is happening in the moment and the laws that govern this whole unfolding, living process.

According to the Buddha, one aspect of right understanding is the essential, underlying wisdom that wholesome and unwholesome actions bring about their respective results. This understanding constitutes the foundation of the entire Dharma. It is the source point for every kind of happiness. When we acquire this basic wisdom— that actions of body, speech, and mind lead somewhere, that they are conditions for different kinds of results—we win the all-important possibility of making wise choices.

We choose wisely simply by cultivating the ability to look at ourself honestly, at our own particular package of qualities, both the wholesome and the unwholesome. The choice is expressed when we practice letting go of, abandoning, not acting on unskillful thoughts and feelings, knowing with wisdom that they will bring unhappiness to ourself and others. In the same way we can choose to act on skillful thoughts and feelings, knowing with wisdom that it will bring happy results. Because of this basic right understanding that actions bring results, we can actually create our life, rather than being victimized or bound by patterns of conditioning.

How does this fashioning of our life work in practice? When we know, for example, that greed is unskillful, that it brings unhappiness, then thoughts of letting go, renunciation, and generosity begin to arise in our mind. From these thoughts come feelings of loving-kindness, compassion, and joy, feelings of wanting to benefit others, to remove their suffering, and to enjoy their happiness.

From understanding that greed is unskillful, and from the thoughts and feelings that follow, we become less self-centered in our life, and these thoughts and feelings then become the condition for actions of generosity and service. The acts of a generous heart strengthen feelings of love and compassion even further, freeing our mind from the suffering of stinginess, selfishness, and pride. Thus through this natural chain of events, we become happier.

It is easy for us to understand the role of natural physical laws, such as the law of gravity or the laws of thermodynamics. The Buddha saw that there is a natural moral law at work as well, influencing the experiences of life. He called it the law of karma, which is just this understanding that actions bring results. This principle is found in many spiritual traditions. Perhaps the most commonly recognized example for us in the West is the biblical saying that we reap what we sow.

The Buddha identified karma as volitional activity. That is, each volition in the mind is like a seed with tremendous potential. In the same way that the smallest acorn contains the potential of a great oak tree, so too each of our willed actions contains the seed of karmic results. The particular result depends on the qualities of mind associated with each volition. Greed, hatred, and delusion are unwholesome qualities that produce fruits of suffering; generosity, love, and wisdom are wholesome factors that bear fruits of happiness.

The Buddha called the understanding of this law of karma, the law of action and result, "the light of the world," because it illuminates how life unfolds and why things are the way they are. The wisdom of this understanding allows us the freedom to make wise choices in our life.

Obvious Karma

If you think too much about karma, you will go crazy, the Buddha warned bluntly. It is too vast. Only a Buddha can understand its scope and intricacies. How can you and I see and grasp how something that happened five lifetimes ago brings results in this life? The interaction of causes and effects in our existence is complex, subtle, and comprehensive. So the law of karma is not just, as popular culture believes, "You do this, and then that happens."

Nonetheless there are familiar, obvious ways we can begin to understand karma. Often we can experience quite immediate results. What is it like when your mind is filled with a variety of mind states or emotions? What does it feel like, for example, to be suffused with joy? Or filled with rage? When we feel such things, we are receiving immediate karmic feedback: the mind state conditions our present experience.

In addition to the feelings themselves, the mind states often bring about speech and action. And actions create reaction. What is likely to happen if you kick a sleeping grizzly? That would be the law of karma at work. What responses are we likely to get if we treat people with kindness, clarity, and honesty? Or if we treat them with rudeness, blaming, deception? In such simple, obvious ways every day our mind states affect what we say and do and bring us quick karmic results.

We also experience the law of karma by reliving past experiences, both wholesome things and unwholesome things. How many times have you reexperienced, sometimes with agonizing vividness, some past deed you regret? Have you ever wished that you could turn the clock back and do it over, with a different result? Conversely, we have all relived in memory deeds we are glad to have done, feeling grateful that we seized the chance for an act of kindness or a time of stillness. Have you ever said, for example, or heard someone else say, "I'm so glad I told her I loved her before she died"?

As we experience the pain or the happiness that derives from present mind states or past actions, we see that no mental event or outward action ends in itself; it leaves an impact or imprint in the mind. Those consequences demonstrate the law of karma. This is not the whole picture, but still we begin to see that cause and effect is not just a spiritual concept; to a large extent, it is what we *are*.

Subtleties of Karma

The idea of karma and the term itself grow more and more common in our language and culture. Once as I was sitting down in an airplane in San Francisco, I found an envelope full of money in the seat pocket in front of me. When I went up to a flight attendant to return the money, she thanked me and said, "Oh, you've made some good karma." So there seems to be some general sense of its meaning, either in doing a good or bad act, or in experiencing some happy or unhappy result.

But there are many subtleties in understanding the law of karma and many ways in which it can be misunderstood. Sometimes people feel that this law of moral cause and effect is deterministic or fatalistic, as if we were bound and powerless in a completely mechanistic system. This is not an accurate understanding, because our actions do not bring about predetermined results. Rather, each action is a seed, and the seed will bear some fruit, but what that particular fruit will be depends on many different conditions interacting in extraordinarily subtle and complex ways.

For example, one of the conditions that determine the karmic result of a past action is the present state of our mind and its ongoing, habituated states. When our mind is generally free from greed, hatred, and ignorance, then unwholesome actions of the past have less opportunity to come to fruition. We are, as it were, protected by the energy field of present wholesomeness; the purity of our minds blocks or modifies those unwholesome karmic results. Likewise, if anger, hatred, fear, greed, or delusion fill our mind habitually, those qualities create the field for past unwholesome actions to bear fruit, and they block or modify the fruits of past wholesome actions.

Our lives are an ongoing, dynamic system in which our current actions continually feed into and alter the unfolding process of past conditioning. We do not know when any seed will come to fruition. We can experience the karmic results of our actions in this lifetime, in the next life, or at any time in the future. But our present actions influence which karmic seeds have the opportunity to come to fruition.

Here is a story that shows how complex and subtle the karmic process can be. In order to find the story credible, you may have to expand or alter your vision of reality. If you do not find it credible, no matter; you do not have to accept any of the Buddhist cosmology in order to attain full liberation.

There was a man during the lifetime of the Buddha who was routinely cruel and unskillful, a miserable creature. He murdered, he stole, he cheated, he deeply habituated harmful mind states in his consciousness and harmful speech and actions in his life. A good candidate for rebirth in a painful realm, right? Ordinarily, yes. But this cruel blackguard did manage to do one very good deed in his life: he offered some food to Sariputra, a fully enlightened being who was the Buddha's chief disciple.

After a life of miserable actions, the law finally caught up with this criminal and sentenced him to hang for his bad deeds. As he stood on the scaffold with the noose around his neck, he happened to see a Buddhist monk walking by. The monk reminded him of his offering food to Sariputra, and he felt joy from that remembrance of giving to such a radiant being.

At that very moment the man hanged. The beneficent power of that last moment—the wholesomeness of that one good deed and the joy that came to him when he recollected it—conditioned the next moment, the moment of rebirth, and he found himself in a very unlikely place. He had been reborn in one of the deva worlds, the celestial realms characterized by happiness and very pleasant experiences.

Imagine his surprise. This criminal had lived a deplorable, cruel life, and here he was, reborn in pleasure groves with everything beautiful! It is said that devas have the power to remember past lives. So, curious, he looked back, saw all the unskillful things he had done, saw his one good act and its recollection at the moment of his death, and understood the karmic effect of that last moment.

Fortunately—so many of these stories of the Buddha's time have happy endings—this ex-criminal celestial being was inspired to undertake Dharma practice. He really worked at it, because he knew that as long as he was in the deva worlds, he would live beyond the reach of his unwholesome karma; it would have no power to reach to that realm. But it would remain, dormant and still potent, the many results of his past harmful actions.

If this deva in delightful realms had not practiced, at the end of his deva life that unwholesome karma would have again borne fruit, probably in one of the lower worlds where there is great pain and suffering. But, seeing this whole situation, he practiced with ardency, became enlightened, and thereby freed himself from the effects of those past actions.

Apropos this wonderful story, the late Venerable Mahasi Sayadaw of Burma, one of the great meditation masters and scholars of the twentieth century, wrote that people who practice sincerely, even if they do not become enlightened in this life, are likely to be reborn in the deva realms. The great good karma of following the precepts and practicing meditation will bring them that benefit. Because the body is luminous, the mind keen, and the intelligence sharp in the deva worlds, those who have had a background of practice in the last life can come to enlightenment very quickly there.

You might recall this good news during those inevitable times when you become discouraged in your practice and may feel tempted to give it up. Your efforts may have effects far beyond anything you imagine.

So the law of karma is very complex. If you feel confused or put off by such complexity, there is one simple fact you can remember: how karmic results unfold for you depends a great deal on the situation you find yourself in right now, on your present mental states. What state are you cultivating in this moment? This question is consequential, because the answer will have powerful influence on how your past actions will bear fruit.

Ignorance, the Root of Harming

When harm is done, who or what is ultimately responsible?

A teacher of a friend of mine was a Hindu *sadhu,* or renunciate, a beautiful man. Years ago he visited America and said something that has stuck with me ever since. He said that when he looks at the world, he does not see cruelty, he does not see war, and he does not see hatred. What he sees is ignorance.

That is what is really happening. All of the harmful actions that people do, all of the things that cause suffering—where are they rooted? They are rooted in deep ignorance, in not understanding the suffering being caused, and not understanding the karmic fruits being created for themselves in doing such actions.

A person walking toward a fire is doing the very thing that will cause the person to be burned. Because of the universal and unavoidable law of karma, when someone does something harmful, if we can see past the action to its root cause in ignorance, then instead of our more usual reaction of anger we can respond with compassion. That person is walking toward the fire of some kind of suffering, the sure result of his or her action.

It does not make sense to feel hatred for ignorance. It neither helps the ignorance nor alleviates the suffering; it only compounds harm with more harm. What helps ignorance is bringing wisdom and compassion to bear on the situation. Brian Keenan, a British hostage released from Lebanon after more than four years in captivity, expressed this basic wisdom. He said that he had no desire for vengeance because vengeance is self-maiming, and he did not intend to maim himself.

I do not mean to imply that we should condone harmful actions. Often strong, decisive responses may be necessary and appropriate. But *how* we respond to such actions depends on how we understand them. It is useful to remember, too, that our responses themselves are likely to generate karmic results to ourselves. When we see clearly that unwholesome actions have their root cause in ignorance, we can then apply our energy to uprooting that cause in ourselves and in others. Compassion feels the suffering caused by ignorance, and wisdom understands what to do.

Mindfulness, the Root of Happiness

Sometimes people have the idea that enlightenment comes when we clear up our karma. According to this notion, we sit and experience the fruit of all of our past actions until we clear it out. Then when our karma is all cleared up, enlightenment happens.

This is a mistaken view, because we are all trailing an infinite amount of past karma. The Buddha said that there is no beginning to be found to the cycle of birth, death, and rebirth of beings. Each of us has lived inconceivable numbers of times, creating inconceivable quantities of skillful and unskillful actions and results. So there is no way actually to clear out all our past karmic fruits. That is not the process we are engaged in.

The key to our freedom comes from two essential things. First, we make an effort to stop causing harm through our speech and actions, so that we stop creating new unwholesome karma that will bring painful results. And second, we learn how to relate skillfully in the present to karmic results from the past.

For example, a painful feeling in the body is a karmic fruit of some past action. If we react to it with aversion, dislike, or hatred, we just create more unwholesome karmic seeds that will bear yet more fruits in the future. But if we relate to that pain with mindfulness, acceptance, softness, and openness, then we are still experiencing the painful result of some past action, but without recreating new unwholesome karma. In the same way, when pleasant feelings arise due to past wholesome karma, we learn to be with them but without attachment or clinging. Through mindfulness of feelings, we stop the reconditioning process. The freedom we can cultivate, the freedom that comes from moment-to-moment awareness in our practice, is the ability to be aware of these changing phenomena without reacting to them, without holding on.

If we can open ourselves, allow ourselves to feel whatever it is without reaction in our mind, then there is no problem. We are fully present for whatever appears without the unwholesome karmic factors of greed, hatred, or ignorance. Thereby we create the conditions for our happiness.

But opening ourselves, especially to very deep-rooted patterns, being mindful of them, means something very specific. It does not mean a superficial or trivial kind of awareness. It does not mean a simple recognition, "Oh yes, I see that pattern." The power of mindfulness as a force in the mind lies in awareness of what is present without identifying with the experience, without identifying with the knower. That is where the freedom is.

So what we practice in every moment is awareness of the breath, thoughts, sensations, emotions, and mind states. Much of this experience comes to us in the present as the result of our past actions. Whatever the experience may be, whether pleasant or unpleasant, is fine if we develop that strength of awareness that can see it, feel it, be with it, without grasping, without aversion, without identifying with it.

After the Buddha's enlightenment, he and the order of monks and nuns were invited to stay in a village during a rainy season. There happened to be famine in that place, and for the three months of the rainy season all they were offered was horse feed for food. The privation was severe. That discomfort was a karmic fruit of some past actions, even for someone as purified as the Buddha. But because of his great wisdom and equanimity, that very difficult situation did not cause any suffering in his mind.

As we respond to the karmic results of past actions with equanimity, without reaction, we bring our mind into greater and greater balance. Enlightenment does not happen because we have gotten rid of a certain amount of karmic activity. It happens when our mind cuts through delusion. And that can occur in any moment; there is no particular time for it.

In an earlier chapter I recounted the story of a man in the Buddha's time called Angulimala, "Garland of Fingers." Even though Angulimala had in the past killed 999 people in cruel ways, he then practiced with great fervor, and in a short time he became fully liberated.

Instead of clearing up all the painful results of his actions, Angulimala cut through the ignorance in his mind and became completely free. Even after he was fully enlightened, as he walked in the villages for alms rounds, people would often throw sticks and stones at him.

All kinds of injuries were done to him as the result of his past actions. But in Angulimala's case, he bore it all with great equanimity,
because his mind was freed.

I like this story because it gives some encouragement when we
get lost in worrying about our own past unskillful actions. Our
awakening does not depend on clearing out all our past karma. It
depends on the quality of our awareness, of balance and wisdom in
the moment.

Karma and No-Self

One of the great interlocking understandings of Buddhadharma links the law of karma with the fundamental principle of emptiness of self. On the surface these two appear contradictory: If there is no self, if there is no single being who carries on through a life, or from life to life, who, then, experiences karmic results? Who is it that dies and is reborn? Although the law of karma and the truth of emptiness seem to contradict, as you investigate further, you see that these two aspects of the Dharma are in fact part of the same whole.

The law of karma is a moral law of cause and effect. It means that actions motivated by different particular factors in the mind bring about different results. It is like planting different seeds in the ground. If you plant an apple seed, you get an apple tree; you do not get a mango. If you plant a mango seed, then you get a mango tree.

Although a seed will bear a particular fruit, clearly the seed itself is not the fruit, nor is the seed somehow carried into the fruit. Rather, a process of transformation is happening according to certain laws. The seed grows into a sapling, the sapling into a tree. The tree bears fruit, which brings forth new seed. That first seed is not pulled up through the trunk and then deposited in the fruit, miraculously splitting into all those other little seeds. Rather, the seed undergoes a process of transformation due to certain conditions, such as sun, rain, and fertile soil.

There is no one element that remains static throughout this process; rather, one thing becomes another, becomes another, continuously. What actually happens in the great unfolding from seed to fruit to seed again is an unbroken continuum of becoming, of ceaseless change. In fact, these changes are happening so rapidly and so continuously that to isolate any one moment and to call it a thing already solidifies too much and renders too static what is so dynamic and transformational.

All of the elements of our own mind and body are arising and passing away, changing continuously, transforming in exactly the same way. To say that there is no self means that there is no permanent entity that carries over from lifetime to lifetime, or even from moment to moment.

What we call self is simply this changing process. In this process, every volitional action is a seed, and the kind of seed it is depends on the quality of mind associated with that volition. These actions bring results in the same way that seeds bear fruit. There is no static "someone," no self, behind these changing events to whom it is all happening. The Buddha described what we are as "actions without an actor, doings without a doer." So we can understand the unfolding of our lives as being a lawful, nonpersonal process of change, a process of constant becoming.

What happens, then, at the time of death? According to the Abhidharma, the Buddhist analysis of mind and body, death consciousness is the last mind-moment of this life. The quality of that moment conditions the arising of rebirth consciousness, the first mind-moment of the new rebirth. There is no *thing*, no self, that is carried over from one life to the next. Just as each moment within this life conditions the next, the mind at the time of death conditions the next moment of rebirth.

Sometimes people feel that the understanding of no-self in this unfolding process somehow absolves us from responsibility for our actions, but that is not an accurate conclusion. Precisely because the law of karma is such a powerful force in our lives, we need to take great care with the actions we perform. They will bear the fruit of either happiness or suffering. The great sage Padmasambhava, who brought Buddhism from India to Tibet, said that although his view is as vast as the sky, his attention to the law of karma is as fine as a grain of barley flour. So even as we understand the selflessness of this living process, we still take care with the actions of our lives.

Animals

Do animals, like humans, also create karma? We can see clearly that animals are conscious, with feelings, awareness, responses, reactions. For that reason, beings in the animal realm create karma as well.

For the most part, though, the animal world does not display much mindfulness. Animals operate mostly on the instinctive level of mind, without the option that mindfulness provides to consider whether an action is skillful or unskillful. Most probably they do not even have such concepts as skillful and unskillful.

The human birth is so precious precisely because we do have the opportunity to discern skillful from unskillful. We have the chance to understand the law of karma, to know that all actions bring results, to bring a moment of consideration to our actions, to make wise choices.

It is interesting to watch our own lives, seeing the range of responses we make to different life situations, to watch when we run on automatic, just moving out of habit and conditioning, without much mindfulness of what we do. Desire arises, and our hand is in the refrigerator. How often does that happen? When we become more aware, bringing mindfulness to bear on our actions through the day, it opens up possibilities of real freedom of choice.

Karma works in all the realms of existence because consciousness, intentions, actions are there. But only when there is mindfulness do we begin to exercise the choice for freedom.

Seven
Practice in the World

Staying Present

How can we remain present and mindful when we move from a meditation sitting or a meditation retreat to our other activities in the world? Making that crucial transition from awareness on the cushion to awareness of daily activities fundamentally affects our freedom.

Practicing mindfulness of the body is one of the easiest ways to stay present in daily life. This mode of awareness works so well that the Buddha devoted many teachings to it. He said that mindfulness of the body leads to nirvana, to freedom, to the unconditioned. So though this practice is very simple, it is in no way trivial or superficial.

Our body is quite obvious as an object of attention, not subtle like thoughts or emotions. We can stay aware of the body easily, but only if we remember to do so. The remembering is difficult, not the awareness.

Remember to use your body as a vehicle for awakening. It can be as simple as staying mindful of your posture. You are probably sitting as you read this book. What are the sensations in your body at this moment? When you put the book down and stand, feel the movements of standing, of walking to the next activity, of how you lie down at the end of the day. Be *in* your body as you move, as you reach for something, as you turn. It is as simple as that.

Staying present in the body is one reason that walking meditation has been so helpful to my own practice. After doing it for thousands of hours over many years, it actually becomes quite natural to feel the movement of my feet and legs as I walk. That habitual presence with the sensations of walking grounds my awareness in other parts of everyday life.

You do not have to practice walking meditation, or any other mindfulness of the body, for hundreds or thousands of hours to feel the benefit. Just patiently practice feeling what is there—and the body is *always* there—until it becomes second nature to know even the small movements you make. If you are reaching for something, you are doing it anyway; there is nothing extra you have to do.

Simply notice the reaching. You are moving. Can you train yourself to be there, to feel it?

It is very simple. Practice again and again bringing your attention back to your body. This basic effort, which paradoxically is a relaxing back into the moment, gives us the key to expanding our awareness from times of formal meditation to living mindfully in the world. Do not underestimate the power that comes to you from feeling the simple movements of your body throughout the day.

Another way to develop a strong investigative mind outside of sitting practice and meditation retreats is to pay particular attention when your experience becomes intense or difficult. Some of our most incisive moments of opening and insight can come at times of difficulty—physical pain, illness, emotional turmoil, danger, any of those moments of heightened experience that come to us all.

Simply because an event is strong, because it naturally rivets our attention anyway, we have a good moment to look carefully, precisely. We bring investigation to bear on what is happening and on our response to it. Am I getting caught? How am I getting hooked? What is skillful means in this situation? Where can I open more or let be?

A legend says that long ago a Buddhist monk was caught by a tiger in the jungle. His fellow monks were unable to help him physically, but from a distance they yelled encouragement to him: "Stay aware! Pay attention!" It is said that, in the extraordinary intensity of being mauled, pulled down, and eaten, this monk attained all the stages of enlightenment in rapid succession before he died.

I do not particularly recommend that you go into the jungle looking for hungry tigers in order to advance quickly on the path! All too often, in one form or another, the tigers come to us. Then it is simply a question of whether we will use them to spiritual advantage or not. If we do not, we may condition ourself more deeply in habitual patterns that keep us in bondage. If we do, then strong experiences can serve as boosters that propel us to liberation.

Wisdom and Love

Wisdom and love are the two great wings of Dharma. Whether we are in the swirl of a busy life or in the deep, still silence of retreat, a clear mind and an open heart are the paramount forces we cultivate as both the means and the end of our path.

These wonderful qualities of mind and heart are not the exclusive virtues of renunciates and Asian masters. They are universal powers, and they show up in the most unlikely places. In some ways, an active layperson's life provides us with continual opportunities for not only cultivating but also manifesting wisdom and love.

One of my first meditation teachers, whom I have mentioned before in these pages, brought love and wisdom together in the most remarkable way. Dipa Ma, an extraordinary woman who lived and taught in Calcutta, was born early in this century and died in 1989. Following the custom of her place and time, she was married at a very early age, around fourteen, and had three children. Then quite suddenly her husband and two of her children died, leaving her in overwhelming grief. She became so debilitated by grief that she was bedridden for several years.

At the time of her husband's and children's deaths, Dipa Ma was living in Burma, where her husband had been in the civil service. After years of disability and decline, she realized that unless she did something to heal her mind and heart, she would surely die. So she went to one of the many Buddhist monasteries in Burma and began meditation practice. Although Dipa Ma's body was small and wasted, she possessed a heart and mind of great strength and power. Within a very short time she attained both high stages of enlightenment and unusually deep powers of concentration.

Dipa Ma's spiritual attainments were quite extraordinary. But what most characterized her life after she began practice was the profound simplicity of her being. Out of this simplicity came the most beautiful integration of the wisdom of emptiness, the fullness of love, and the stillness of unshakable peace. Once when Dipa Ma was asked what was in her mind, she replied, "Concentration, lovingkindness, and peace. That is all."

In this statement you can see integration at work. The peace came from uprooting defilements, those qualities of greed, hatred, and ignorance that cause turbulence and torment in our mind. Uprooting these defilements came from mindfulness. Dipa Ma often used the lovingkindness practice to develop deep states of concentration, and then used deep concentration to develop insight and wisdom through the power of mindfulness.

Within Dipa Ma all these qualities cultivated in practice fed into one another. Lovingkindness fed into insight. Insight then became a basis for freedom from defilements, and this allowed her mind to become more concentrated, making the power of lovingkindness even stronger. It was beautiful to see. In Dipa Ma's presence, one felt that love and wisdom had become one.

Dipa Ma has been an important model for me and others because she carried on her powerful practice very much in the world, as householder, mother, and grandmother. She never relaxed her effort to attain the final goal, though she made that effort in an open, loving, and generous way. So next time you feel that your work or parenting or a relationship or some worldly tangle is holding up your spiritual practice, you might remember Dipa Ma and make those very things your practice.

Lovingkindness

In his book *Love's Executioner,* the well-known Stanford psychiatrist Irwin Yalom writes: "I do not like to work with patients who are in love. Perhaps it is because of envy. I, too, crave enchantment. Perhaps it is because love and psychotherapy are fundamentally incompatible. The good therapist fights darkness and seeks illumination, while romantic love is sustained by mystery and crumbles upon inspection. I hate to be love's executioner."

Is there a kind of love that does not crumble on inspection, that is compatible with and enhances illumination? Is there a difference between the enchantment of *falling in love* and that quality of being when we are *standing in love*? This special quality in Pali is called *metta,* lovingkindness.

Metta is generosity of the heart that wishes happiness to all beings, both oneself and others. Lovingkindness softens the mind and heart with feelings of benevolence. The mind becomes pliable and the heart gentle as metta seeks the welfare and benefit of all. The feeling of lovingkindness expresses the simple wish "May you be happy."

Because we react less and remain more open when we cultivate metta, the softness and pliability of love become the ground for wisdom. We see with greater clarity what is wholesome and skillful in our life and what is not. As this discriminating wisdom grows, we make wiser life choices that lead us again to greater happiness and more love.

In a beautifully interrelated way, mindfulness creates the field in which metta grows. We first collect the attention and gather the scattered mind. In the beginning of mindfulness practice, we may be distracted or overcome by hindrances. But slowly awareness works its magic. We observe, come back from being lost, begin again, and gradually our mind becomes more accepting, less reactive, and less judgmental. We do not get so totally lost in discursive thoughts. A soft and gentle awareness allows our mind and heart to relax, to loosen, to open.

This opening often invites a stream of memories and images, at first from the recent past, and then from even long-forgotten circumstances. A vast reservoir of impressions and reactions reveals itself. We may think of people, or remember incidents, we have not thought of in years. Through the growing power of a still and focused mind, we experience these thoughts and feelings with great clarity and immediacy; in our mind we begin to reconnect with people in our life.

At first, these memories may carry old reactions and judgments, but as our mind becomes quieter, we remember people and situations with less projection and less defensiveness. The stillness of a silent mind allows a greater vulnerability and tenderness. We see more clearly other sides of people and situations, and we can often forgive more easily. In this soft, open space of awareness, feelings of lovingkindness and compassion begin to arise more and more spontaneously.

The feeling of metta makes no distinction among beings. When love is mixed with desire, there is some energy of wanting, and therefore the love always remains limited. We may desire one, or two, or perhaps three people, but I think there has never been desire for all beings in the world. Unlike desire, metta has the capacity to embrace all; no one lies outside its sphere. People with this feeling of love are always blessing: "Be happy, be healthy, live in safety, be free."

Because lovingkindness comes from the generosity of our heart and does not depend on conditions or people being a certain way, it does not change easily into ill will. There are many stories of Ryokan, the hermit monk and poet of eighteenth-century Japan, that illustrate this nondiscrimination. One of them tells of a thief going to Ryokan's little hut and stealing his few possessions. When Ryokan returned and saw what had happened, he wrote this haiku:

> The thief left it behind—
> the moon
> At the window.

How would we be in the same situation?

The power of the Buddha's teaching comes from the repeated reminder that love and wisdom are qualities not simply to admire in others but also to practice and develop in ourself. Thich Nhat Hanh, the Vietnamese meditation master, poet, and peace activist, wrote: "Practicing Buddhism is a clever way to enjoy life. Happiness is available. Please help yourself to it."

How can we help ourselves to love? Focusing on the good qualities in people, both ourselves and others, causes the feeling of metta to arise. We are all a package of different qualities. When we do not see the good in a person and concentrate instead on what we do not like, then it becomes easy for ill will, anger, judgments, and even hatred to arise. We do not pretend that unwholesome qualities are absent; rather, we can see and understand them without our mind dwelling on those characteristics. Everyone has at least one good quality. When we seek out this good quality in a person, then a feeling of loving regard grows quite naturally. At first this way of relating to people may seem artificial or contrived, but over time lovingkindness becomes our natural way of living.

Metta also grows from feelings of gratitude. In a striking commentary on human relationships, the Buddha said that two things are remarkably rare in this world: people who benefit others, and people who feel gratitude. We have all been helped by others in so many ways. To reflect on the good things that different people have done for us nurtures the feelings of genuine gratitude and love.

Another way to strengthen metta is through lovingkindness meditation. This practice is very simple. Sit comfortably, think of a person for whom you already feel a lot of love, and silently repeat a few phrases that express that love. For example, you might repeat the phrases "May you be happy," "May you be healthy," "May you live in safety," "May you be free." Let the mind rest a few moments in the meaning and feeling of each phrase as you hold the person in mind. Then go on to the next phrase.

As you practice this meditation, gradually the feeling of metta grows strong. You can then bring to mind a good friend, a neutral person, and even someone with whom you have experienced difficulty, what is traditionally called an "enemy." Be patient in the practice. Slowly we retrain the habits of our heart. You might end the metta meditation expressing loving wishes to all beings: "May all beings be happy, be healthy, live in safety, be free."

Metta is a force, dynamic and transformative, that can change our whole experience of life. You can practice it in your casual contacts with people. When you walk down the street notice the difference between the isolation of being lost in your own business and the feelings of connection when you inwardly repeat the phrases of lovingkindness. An immediate transformation takes place as we hold the space of the street and its people in an energy field of metta. You can practice lovingkindness for the people you are closest to. You can practice it for all beings in this world.

Compassion

Love expresses itself in another way that is as powerfully transformative as metta. Just as metta sees the good in beings and wishes for their happiness, compassion is the kind of love that sees the suffering of beings and wishes for their release from it.

Compassion—*karuna* in Pali and Sanskrit—is the strong feeling of wanting to alleviate pain and suffering. The Buddha described this feeling as a quivering or tenderness of the heart. Compassion arises when we come close to suffering, when we open to and feel the suffering either in ourself or others.

In the busyness of our daily routines, we often create a wall of distraction that dulls the immediacy of difficult or painful feelings. Although at times this might be a useful strategy, it potentially also dulls the feeling of compassion within us.

A meditation retreat can be a powerful place to develop compassion because we find ourself face to face with a wide range of feelings in our own body and mind. The great gift of silence creates a space of nondistraction, so we actually feel the suffering that is there, both in ourself and in the world.

Over a period of time, meditation develops a tremendous tenderness of heart. Although it is not always apparent in the day-to-day hindrances and ups and downs of practice, a softening of the mind and heart takes place that transforms the way we relate to ourselves and to others. We begin to feel more deeply, and this depth of feeling becomes the wellspring of compassion.

Subtleties of understanding engender important consequences in how we live. For example, understanding the difference between opening to suffering and feeling aversion to it can make the difference between living with compassion and living with fear. Sometimes we feel that we are open, because we know the suffering is there. But knowing is not enough. We often know with aversion, or resistance, or judgment. You can see for yourself the difference between openness and aversion in the very simple and common experience of being with physical pain. Sometimes our mind accepts the pain with interest and a willingness to explore. At other times we tighten or turn away in aversion to the painful feeling. These are two very different states. Compassion never comes from turning away from suffering. The strong compassionate feeling to alleviate suffering comes from our willingness to be with it.

Meditation practice enables us to see the whole world in our own mind and body. We see all the noble qualities that are found in the world, and we see all the qualities that make for suffering and war and conflict. We find it all inside ourselves. For example, a mosquito comes and buzzes around your ear. It comes closer and closer. What do you feel? Instead of feeling compassion for the mosquito, you probably want to swat it. We have all experienced this kind of re-action. Yet on a very small scale, these are the same seeds of action that play out in the world in so many disastrous ways. We encounter something that we do not like, something unpleasant, something threatening, and we want to do away with it. For us the swat is a simple movement of the hand; for the mosquito it is quite a momentous event.

In many small, everyday situations we can watch and observe this tendency toward aversion. If we do not see it, if we delude ourselves that we do not have those feelings, then we have no chance at all of freeing ourselves from their grip. We then just act them out unconsciously in our lives. The mosquito buzzes. Can we hear the sound, know the feeling and thoughts that arise in the mind, see the desire to call in the SWAT team, and be aware enough to exercise compassion?

Here is another story about the monk Ryokan. He would spend his days wandering through the mountain villages, playing with children and living a life of simplicity and compassion. One warm spring day, it is said, he picked the lice from his robe and placed them on a rock to sun themselves. At the end of the day, as night began to fall, he took them from the rock and placed them back on his robe! We may not all be Ryokan, but mindfulness and understanding provide those moments when we can touch compassion within us.

How many times in your life have you turned away from a newscast, a homeless person on the street, or even some demands on your time from a friend seeking your support, because the suffering you encounter seems too much to allow into your consciousness? Next time that happens, and you have enough awareness to see it happening, try changing the mental weather in your heart.

Try gently to drop aversion to the pain, and just open to it. Open to the one or the ones in suffering. Allow the feeling of separation from that being or beings to dissolve. And then notice how your heart feels. Even though you are encountering suffering, a kind of happiness has come. It is not the suffering itself that causes our discomfort; rather, it is our aversion to it and our sense of separation from others. When those go, the discomfort goes. Even though it encompasses anguish and pain, compassion is an empowering joy.

Compassion can also be practiced as a specific meditation. Think of a person in difficulty, and as you hold him or her in your mind, gently repeat the phrase "May you be free from suffering." As your mind concentrates more and more deeply on the person and on the repetition of the phrase, the feeling of compassion flowers within you. You can then extend this feeling to groups of people, and finally, to all beings everywhere.

The Art of Communication

During periods of meditation practice, whether for an hour each day or for longer retreats, we stay mostly in silence. But when we live our daily lives, we are in active communication much of the time. What proportion of your life do you spend talking or writing? Notice how much impact your words have on others, and theirs on you. Because speech is so predominant in our lives, and because our words are so consequential, learning the art of skillful communication needs to be a significant aspect of our Dharma practice.

The Buddha emphasized the importance of this when he included right speech as a distinct part of the path to awakening. Although there is great elaboration of right speech in the texts, it all condenses into two general principles: Is it true? Is it useful?

Practicing these principles in our speech fosters increasing sensitivity. We become attuned to subtleties of truth and falsehood. Are there times when we shade the truth, or exaggerate in some way? And are there times when our words may be true, but it is not the right time, place, or situation for them to be useful.

The practice of communication is the great art of relating to another person, of being open, of listening so well that you can see where you can actually make contact. Can you let the other person in? What is the right vocabulary? Can you speak to what is really important to that person? We learn to listen and speak from a feeling of metta, basic goodwill. Wise discernment and metta enable us to connect.

There are always two parts in any interaction. One part is to learn how to speak effectively, and the other is to learn how to listen effectively. Remembering to listen seems especially important in times of difficult communication, when there is tension or conflict. Other people always have their own point of view. If we want to truly connect with and understand others, we must also listen.

When you are in a confrontation with someone and you are each very attached to your own perspective, ideas, and feelings, see if you can find a moment to take a mental step back and say, "Okay, let me try to understand this from another vantage point." This helpful change requires a great ability to listen. From there genuine communication may begin to happen.

This does not mean that you do not express your own understanding. You can, but from that space of openness where it becomes much easier to speak without aggression. If you are able first to listen, already the ground between you and the other person has changed.

Sometimes we take that step, but the situation proves out of our control. Sometimes the space does not open up despite our efforts, and the lack of communication does not change. That is when we really need to stay centered in ourselves, in our bodily awareness, so that we do not become caught again in our reaction to what is happening. At such difficult times we can draw on the wisdom of our meditation practice: to see that it is possible to open to unpleasant feelings, to see that it is okay simply to feel them instead of reacting with defensiveness or aggression.

As you soften and make space around these feelings, the reactions of mind come and go more easily, without your staying locked in them. This skill takes a lot of practice. If you have not practiced it before, in the midst of an intense communication you will at first find it difficult to do.

So our job in practice is to look at how we relate to our feelings. Anger comes, annoyance comes, fear comes—both in sitting and in our daily communications these feelings come. Can you be mindful of them all? Or is there a strong identification with those emotions?

The truth that anger and fear are not inherently tied to external situations runs counter to our "commonsense," conventional conditioning. But look closely for yourself to see if it is true. We feed these unwholesome feelings by blaming. The more we blame, the more we strengthen anger and resentment in ourselves. But if mindfulness and investigation are strong enough, we can unhook from the identification.

If we practice such unhooking, it then becomes much easier to communicate with people in difficult situations. Because we can communicate from the place of our own mental ease and compassion, our communication becomes much more effective. Can something be changed through communication? Can the person with the boom box play it down the block? Is it possible to say to somebody coming on too strong that what they are doing does not feel right? Can we be firm without anger or blame?

People sometimes confuse acceptance with a wishy-washy way of being in this world: letting anybody do anything, and never taking a stand. That's not it at all. Acceptance means taking responsibility for our own mind states. With mindfulness, it is possible to take a strong stand, to initiate effective communication, yet to do it without getting caught in reactive judgments. The energy with which we communicate is the key.

Sharing the Dharma

All of us who practice the Buddha's way encounter a particular form of communication that can be difficult. Sharing with our family and friends about our Dharma practice, our understanding, is a great art that in itself is a challenging practice.

Faith and confidence are wonderful fruits of practice, but we always have to balance them with discerning wisdom. Sometimes people become so charged with enthusiasm from the fresh energy of a meditation retreat that they want to tell their friends and family all about it. They assume that everyone will be interested. Sometimes people are, and sometimes they are not. Someone may greet you with "How was the retreat?" That may just be their way of saying hello. If you give them a three-hour discourse on the absence of self when they are just saying hello, your discernment may need some adjustment.

Try to remember in such communications, as in all communications, to listen carefully enough to what people are asking so that you know whether they are really interested or are just saying hello. Here is a chance to put your practice to work, to exercise mindfulness and sensitivity. And even when you feel that a person is genuinely interested in learning about your experience, you need to let go of your own agenda in order to use the right skillful means.

With the Dharma any single part contains the whole, like a hologram. Whatever starting place you choose as you communicate with others can unfold to reveal the whole Dharma. This allows for the creativity of intuitive wisdom. You do not have to start at any particular place. Rather, you can open to another's experience and see where that person actually is. What are the concerns? Where is the suffering? Where is the interest? Begin from that place. If you genuinely hear a person, and if your outlook is one of lovingkindness, then there is already an intimacy of connection.

And even when our words feel inadequate, not hitting the mark, remember that the deepest communication is always in the way we are with people, not in what we say. The words we use may or may not connect, but the quality of our presence always communicates. If you are more loving, more accepting, less judgmental, and more compassionate in your relationship with friends and family, that is a powerful communication.

Years ago someone wrote to Ram Dass after studying with him for a while. She had gone home to her family, who were fundamentalist Christians and very opposed to what she was doing. She was having a hard time, and in her letter she described her difficulties. At the very end of it she said, "My parents hate me when I'm a Buddhist, and they love me when I'm a Buddha."

Relationship with Parents

Of all forms of human communication, connecting skillfully to parents can, for many of us in the West, seem the most challenging.

The Buddha said that because our parents made our life and growth possible, we have a special karmic relationship with them. In addition to the actual physical events of conception and birth that brought us life, our parents also gave us an enormous amount of care after we were born, at a time when we could not care for ourselves. Without their protection and support, we could not have survived.

In so many ways our parents gave us the gift of life. Because of this fact, the Buddha spoke of the responsibility we have to care for them in return, and to try to establish them on the path of wisdom. He used a very strong image to convey this point: even if we carried our parents on our shoulders for our entire life, the Buddha said, it would not be enough to repay our debt to them.

In our Western culture this teaching sometimes creates difficulties, because many people have emotional conflicts with or about their parents. They may have unresolved disappointment and anger, and may feel that their parents did not, after all, care for them enough as children. We have even been learning increasingly in recent years that a distressingly high number of children in our society suffer emotional, physical, or sexual abuse by their parents.

It seems as if the traditional Buddhist texts did not have Western culture in mind. For example, one classic teaching from the texts urges us to think of every being as our mother. This advice implies that if you feel toward all beings as you feel toward your mother, you will have unbounded love for them. Clearly this perspective does not always work well, as we in the West often have problems with our parents and with our children.

Coming to a wholesome relationship with our parents may be hard, but it is not impossible. In the early days of my practice in India, I had a friend whose mother was extremely angry that he was there practicing meditation. He would get letters from her saying that she would rather see him in hell than to have him in India meditating. You can imagine the impact of receiving a letter like that from your mother while you are very sensitized by deep, intensive practice. They were fiercely angry letters.

One day we were talking about this situation with Dipa Ma, our teacher in Calcutta. When my friend told her of his mother's letters, Dipa Ma reached under her mattress, took out ten rupees, gave them to him, and said, "Buy her a gift." Dipa Ma lived very simply in Calcutta, so those ten rupees were themselves a consequential gift.

My friend followed her advice. Because he responded not with anger but with generosity, because he did not simply withdraw in response to his mother's wounding letters, that gift began a gradual change in his relationship with her. Her response softened, and their relationship began to heal. The story ends in quite an unusual way. My friend eventually returned to live with both his mother and his father, caring for them full time until they died.

This story interests and inspires me because it shows that even when the relationship is extremely difficult, if we know the importance of keeping an open heart and maintaining contact, the situation can become workable.

It helps to remember that we have a very special karmic relationship to our parents. We were not born into a particular family by accident. No matter what kind of emotional relationship we have had with our parents, in some way or other they made it possible for us to connect to the Dharma. So something worked out beautifully, even if our attraction to the Dharma may have come about as a reaction to great suffering in our lives. There is something wonderful about the way life has unfolded to enable us to hear and practice Dharma—a rare opportunity in the world.

Parents can be a splendid test. We practice on ourselves, then we go home. Here is the final exam! "Oops. Didn't make it that time."

What are some ways to work with situations where our parents are difficult or the relationship is difficult? One of the hardest things is not to expect them to be different from what they are. Relating to people by wanting them to be different creates tension and conflict.

Suppose you have rigid, controlling parents. Have you ever observed a rigid, controlling mind in yourself? We all have many sides to ourselves, and we act them out in different ways. Can we extend to our parents the same acceptance and compassion we try to generate toward everything we see in ourselves—the same nonreactiveness, nonjudgment, and nonevaluation? This does not mean that we have to like rigidity, but we can learn nevertheless to be genuinely accepting and compassionate.

As you relate to difficult parents, you might also remember the proximate cause of metta, or lovingkindness: seeing the good in beings. Even when people have many negative tendencies, almost everyone has at least some endearing qualities. Focus on those things. If you really aim your mind at the good qualities, it will create some feeling of metta.

And, again, no matter how troubled our psychological relationship with our parents has been, or how they have behaved toward us, somebody took care of us when we were entirely unable to fend for ourselves. For most of us, that somebody was one or both of our parents, or caretakers acting as our parents. That is a great gift. They may have had their own uptightness and confusion, but nevertheless we are breathing in this moment because of them. That is why the Buddha emphasized so dramatically the debt we owe to our parents for such extraordinary giving that actually enabled us to stay alive.

We cannot deny that often there are deep problems, and there is no guarantee the problems will change. But even then we can come to a space of acceptance, truly feeling metta and compassion. Coming to that space is a very important part of Dharma practice, because we suffer when we are cut off in a fundamental way from our parents or from anyone. Trying to keep channels of communication open, trying just to be there with the way our parents are, is well worth the effort.

I should add one caveat here. If you are a survivor of abuse, if you suffered physical, sexual, or emotional violence committed by your parents, you may have to go through a necessary process before you can open to them with forgiveness and compassion. True healing and forgiveness, both within ourselves and with others, cannot be achieved by shortcut; first we have to know and understand fully the suffering involved.

So abuse survivors may necessarily have to experience a therapeutic time of thoroughly feeling the fear, the anger, the hatred, and the grief caused by the abuse, and for their healing they may have to go through a period of no contact with those who caused the pain. After completing this process, then they may choose to reach out with forgiveness, love, and acceptance.

In addition to caring for our parents, we can also fulfill our responsibility to them by trying to establish them in the Dharma in some way. We begin this effort simply by being a certain way with them, so that even without words we communicate something strongly. That communication has to come first from our own acceptance of them as people. If you go back to your parents and start talking to them about selflessness and dependent co-arising and tell them they have to meditate every day, it surely will not work. But if you go back and manifest a spirit that is a little more loving, caring, and accepting, then some communication can evolve out of that acceptance. And then it is just a matter of looking for opportunities.

When I first began Dharma practice and was traveling back and forth between America and India, I felt very enthusiastic about meditation. When I was in the United States, I would stay at home with my mother. After dinner I would cut a little deal with her: "How about you meditating while I wash the dishes?" She was happy with that bargain and agreed to try. That was the beginning.

Right Livelihood

We all need food, shelter, and clothing, and we need the means to obtain such necessities. How can we use this unavoidable aspect of life, our livelihood, as part of our practice? The Buddha considered how we make our living so important that he made right livelihood one of the eight aspects of the Eightfold Noble Path, those qualities we must practice and perfect in order to liberate ourselves. So right livelihood is an important question, particularly for those of us practicing in the West.

Most Asian Buddhists deeply committed to liberation enter the monasteries. When you are in a monastery, you do not have a problem about right livelihood; every aspect of your life, down to the smallest detail, has been especially designed to expedite your liberation.

But, at least for now, most of us who follow the Dharma in the West have not chosen to go the monastic route. We live in the world as laypeople, right in the midst of the maelstrom. And yet, at the same time we feel a deep commitment to liberation in this lifetime. We are not just practicing to be reborn in a heaven, or deva, world; we really want to be free.

So how to bring this dedication, interest, and aspiration into our work in the world, outside the monasteries, is a very key question. We are all challenged by this question, and we are discovering the answers right now by living out the problem. Our generation of practitioners will pass on a wisdom forged through a lot of difficulty, because this search for solutions is not an easy one.

From the perspective of right livelihood, it is not essential that we do any particular kind of work, apart from avoiding those activities that are obviously harmful, that involve killing or stealing. Most livelihoods can be part of the spiritual path. It depends less on the work itself than on how we do it.

One story epitomizes for me the spirit we can bring to our work. Years ago the great Tibetan Buddhist teacher Kalu Rinpoche visited the Boston aquarium. As he walked through the aquarium, he tapped on each window of the tanks to get the attention of the fish.

And as the fish swam up to him, he said very quietly, "OM MANI PADME HUM," a blessing in the Tibetan tradition.

Just to go through life blessing others is a beautiful thing to do. Dipa Ma was also like that. She was always blessing. She blessed people and animals and airplanes and buses. Wherever she went, she gave blessings: "Be happy, be happy." If somehow we can practice that spirit of blessing in our work, the spirit of service, then we transform what could be a very ordinary job into something that really carries us along the great way. The power of that spirit is tremendous. Cultivating it takes a presence of mind. Remember that whatever work we do can be an offering of service to others.

The Dalai Lama conveyed this idea very simply:

> We are visitors on this planet. We are here for ninety, a hundred years at the very most. During that period we must try to do something good, something useful with our lives. Try to be at peace with yourself and help others share that peace. If you contribute to other people's happiness, you will find the true goal, the true meaning of life. ∽

On Reading Texts

Because the teachings emphasize the direct, unmediated experience of Dharma, the essential nature of reality, people sometimes feel confused about whether they should read Dharma texts at all. Is it necessary to read and study the texts to come to a deep understanding? The answer is clearly no. Many great saints and sages throughout the centuries have practiced without much study, or have even been illiterate, but have come to profound realization of the Dharma. Can it be helpful to study the texts? For many people, the answer is clearly yes.

The texts themselves are simply the Buddha's teachings, or the teachings of other great masters in the various Buddhist traditions. They point directly to the nature of the mind, the nature of suffering, and the nature of freedom. These teachings are not to be taken simply on belief, but rather they can be used as arrows pointing to our direct experience. When someone points a finger at the moon, the value of the pointing is in our looking at the moon, not in our staring at the finger. For this reason, reading texts does not have to be just an academic investigation. These extraordinary teachings are not merely a system of ideas, nor are they a set of beliefs. They are more basic, more essential than that, illuminating how the mind works, what the nature of reality is, and how to cultivate clarity of perception.

Before beginning meditation practice, reading and studying can clarify the teachings and inspire people to take the next steps on their spiritual journey. And reading the original texts after one has practiced a fair amount can open new doors of understanding. When you read in the proper external and internal environment—when the mind is settled, quiet, concentrated—the words may come alive in an extraordinary way. So if you have done some sitting already, and if you are inclined to do so, you may find that going back to the original sources widens your perspective of the path.

Several of the English translations are not very good. Many sutras, or teachings of the Buddha, contain a lot of repetition because they were transmitted orally for several centuries before they were written down. If you read them expecting to be entertained, Robert

Ludlum would work better. But if you read them slowly and carefully as a direct pointing to reality and take the time to investigate, to taste the nature of that reality, they can illuminate your experience considerably, and clarify and deepen your practice.

Humor

A sense of humor is indispensable in the practice of the Dharma, both on retreat and on the roller coaster of our life in the world. When we reflect for a moment on the quality of mind a sense of humor implies, we see that it creates some inner space. Being able to see the humor, the lightness, and the emptiness of phenomena is really a great blessing during those times when we become caught in the various dramas of our lives.

The Buddhist texts provide a whole explanation of manifestations of humor. They do it, of course, in the traditionally dry fashion of the Abhidharma, the Buddhist psychology. The texts describe the different kinds of laughs people have at various stages along the path. When something strikes uncultured worldlings as being funny, they will roll about on the floor. One in middling stages of enlightenment will laugh out loud. Arhats, or fully enlightened beings, will laugh showing their teeth. And the Buddha simply smiled. The point is that there are refinements to the quality of humor.

Being with different teachers and seeing so many different styles of Dharma teachings and presentations has taught me much about humor, including understanding that humor is often quite a cultural matter. I have seen the most strict and demanding Asian teachers almost lose control laughing at a particular joke that does not seem funny at all from a Western point of view. At one time, the late Burmese master Venerable Taungpulu Sayadaw was giving a Dharma talk. He always lectured in the traditional fashion, holding a ceremonial fan in front of him. He was talking about mind and matter, and one of the yogis asked whether a dog has both. The Sayadaw could hardly stop laughing. He thought that was the funniest question as he reflected on what the alternative might be.

Humor also serves us in times of great difficulty or suffering. It helps create spaciousness of mind around the suffering and can help loosen the bonds of identification. One example of this is Oscar Wilde's probably apocryphal last words. He had been released from prison a sick, broken, impoverished, disgraced, and dying man. He went to Paris, where he died in a cheap rooming house in a slum.

The wallpaper in his rented room was horrendously ugly, and Wilde was nothing if not a stylish man. It is said that just before Wilde died, as he lay on his deathbed, he turned his face to the wall and said, "One of us has got to go."

Training for Death

Next time you face some difficulty, imagine that you face your dying moment; imagine that you are actually dying. How then do you want to relate to the difficulty? From the perspective of the dying moment, are you willing to be lost in confusion and reaction? Do you want to avoid the moment, to hide from it? Or do you want to be accepting, present, and alert?

Many different spiritual traditions emphasize the practice of recollecting our death, because such an awareness puts the events of our life into a powerful perspective. How easily we become caught up, invested in our own dramas and stories. The recollection of death, as a living presence in our life, can bring us out of the movies of our mind and put our experience into a much bigger perspective. By holding that awareness, we live with greater spaciousness and ease.

Thinking of meditation practice as training for dying inspires me a lot, especially in times of emotional storm or physical pain. Probably dying will be difficult. So here we are right now in a difficult situation. We see where we are and how we can open. This is our training.

We sit, and after fifteen or twenty minutes some discomfort comes in the body—pain in the knee, maybe—or in the mind. We see what a struggle it is actually to open in a balanced way to that discomfort. But by practicing it, we learn it.

There is a fair chance that we will face even more discomfort as we die. Probably there will be some measure of pain in the body and some difficult emotions as we begin that incredible journey into the unknown. How will we be able to relate to them? Will we be able to face them from a place of peace, of openness, of acceptance? Or will we react with fear or anxiety, or even with panic or terror?

Every sitting, every walking, every moment that we practice is an opportunity to train our mind. Can I open to this? Can I accept this? And the deeper we go in practice, the closer to the edges we get, those boundaries of what we are willing to be with expand. Death may be such a boundary. Can we train ourself so well that we can cross that boundary with confidence when we come to it?

Vipassana and Death

As we go through this process—whether it is the process of our life or the process of our dying—the power of vipassana, insight meditation, develops a very strong observing power of mind.

Often in the midst of our practice, as we struggle with the ups and downs, the times when things are clear and the times when they are not, we forget the tremendous force and karmic power of every moment of seeing clearly. The Buddha illustrated in a very telling way just how powerful is the work we are doing.

He described the various karmic strengths of different activities. One such activity is *dana,* the Pali word for generosity, a great power of purification that the Buddha emphasized again and again in his teaching.

He said that the karmic power of a gift is determined by three things: the purity of the giver, the purity of the receiver, and the purity of the gift itself—that is, whether or not the thing has been rightfully acquired. So according to this understanding, to make an offering to a fully enlightened being has extraordinary karmic potency because of that person's purity.

The Buddha then said that it is far more consequential to experience *just one moment* of a mind fully absorbed in the feeling of lovingkindness, or metta, than it is to give a gift to the Buddha himself and the entire order of enlightened beings. And further, he said that many times more powerful than a mind fully concentrated on loving feelings is the karmic consequence of one moment's clearly seeing the arising and passing away of phenomena. The Buddha was referring here to that stage of insight in the vipassana practice where one knows very surely the momentariness of all appearances.

This clear and sure insight into impermanence is far more fruitful than giving a gift to the Buddha and the whole order of enlightened beings, or of feeling lovingkindness. Why? Because in that clarity of vision lies the seed of freedom.

What is the alternative? We all experience it often in our lives. We become caught up in, and identified with, different emotions, thoughts, interactions, confusions, various pains in the body and in the mind. At these times we forget the most basic truths of existence and contract into the prison of self.

There may well be physical and mental suffering at the time of your death. Can you train yourself to be with them in an alert, open way, simply noticing, so that you remain as conscious and unentangled as possible? Can you rest in awareness, undistracted, as this great mystery unfolds and see the basic impermanence and insubstantiality of all appearances? If you can encounter the experience of dying with this much mindfulness, then even if there is confusion, fear, or pain, your noticing mind will be so strong that these things will pose no problem: "Oh, just confusion, confusion, fear."

Or will you be lost instead in those habitual reactions of craving, hatred, fear, whatever?

Do you see in this way how the practice we do, this simple, clear observation, is tremendously powerful? Do not undervalue the results of simply staying present with the moment's experience, and of insight into impermanence on a momentary level. The consequences for how we live and how we die are far greater than we may ordinarily realize.

Metta and Death

Metta, lovingkindness, can also be an extraordinary tool for dealing with our own death or with the deaths of others.

Metta has a special power to soften the mind and heart as a way to deal with fear and to overcome it. The oncoming of something as mysterious as death can very often arouse fear in our mind. We may fear the pain that often comes with dying. We may fear the uncertainty of our situation. We may fear the unknown.

When the Buddha first introduced metta meditation, he taught it to a group of monks who were in a terrifying situation as a specific antidote to the mind state of fear. Any of us can have a sense of the power of lovingkindness if we develop it deeply. As the metta becomes strong, we learn to reside longer and longer in a place of goodwill and loving care for ourselves and for other beings. As we rest in the simplicity and strength of these feelings, we see that when metta is in our heart, fear is absent. Metta and fear do not coincide.

The stronger the metta, the more it stands as a bedrock for us. It becomes a refuge. So we gain tremendous strength from cultivating this quality deeply, a strength we can turn to at any crisis in our lives, including our death.

Metta and vipassana are complementary powers that can be blended together skillfully. If in a difficult situation like dying we become too constricted, too reactive, too caught up, and mindfulness is not strong enough in itself to deal with the situation, then we can take refuge in lovingkindness practice until the mind and heart become more peaceful. After some time of resting in ease, we can open again with mindfulness to whatever is present.

Having this skill in blending the two types of meditation is critical for how we practice now, for how we manage at the time of our death, and also for how we are present with others who are dying. A person's surroundings at the time of death can do a lot to support a wholesome mind state. Even if someone dying does not appear to be responsive, do not assume the person is unaware. I have heard many stories of people who have been in comas who, after coming out of them, spoke about having experienced a state of great clarity. They were not communicating, but they were very present. We do not really know what is going on at such times. It may look one way from the outside and be very different on the inside.

We serve a dying person by generating the force of metta. If we can do it in a pure, strong way, it has a calming effect; we radiate the energy of peace.

Vipassana can also serve us wonderfully at such a time because it gives us the power to observe our own mind. Mindfulness enables us to watch the feelings and reactions we are going through, without becoming caught up in them and having our reactions leach into an already difficult situation. Witnessing the dying of someone we care about can be a very intense experience. As difficulties come up for us, can we open to them, let them wash through, and then settle back into the radiant power of lovingkindness?

To Benefit All Beings

Whether we consciously intend to or not, we journey on this path of awakening not only for ourselves but also to benefit all beings. As we begin to understand more deeply our own nature, the reality of mind and body, we see that this nature is universal. We see that differences are relatively superficial; they are differences of certain kinds of conditioning only.

Our personalities are different. So are the look of our bodies and the contents of our thoughts. But the *way* our mind and body works is the same in each of us: anger, fear, love, and compassion feel the same in all people; our bodies all get old and die. From a growing awareness of ourselves, we come to a much deeper sense of our commonality with others.

To the degree that we understand this commonality, we relate to other beings in a very different way. We have much less sense of separation, less sense that other people, and even animals, are so different from us.

I have felt this falling away of separation most noticeably as I have traveled to teach in different cultures. For example, I have taught several times in what was formerly the Soviet Union. Both the living conditions there and how people relate to one another are quite different from here. Yet, in the practice of Dharma, the commonality of experience became so obvious: the same knee pain, the same wandering mind, the same emotions, the same power of awareness. We all saw that underneath the differences of culture and circumstance we shared the basic truths of life. This led, as it always does, to strong feelings of closeness and connection. By understanding ourself, we quite naturally come to understand others, feeling increasingly the bonds of oneness. Issa, a sixteenth-century Japanese poet, expressed this well: "In the cherry blossom's shade, there's no such thing as a stranger."

Our own practice also directly benefits all beings. Precisely because everything is interdependent, we recognize that our life, of necessity, has an effect in this world. There are so many levels of connection among all beings and things that the quality of our mind and heart inevitably has effects that we might not even see.

The new science of chaos describes how underneath our ordinary perception things are very chaotic and hard to understand. This chaos reveals itself to us in such everyday events as weather changes or smoke rising. Yet, if you go deeply into this chaos, you find wonderful patterns and connections within it. There is a principle called "sensitive dependence on initial conditions," which means that a small input at the beginning of a process can result in a large output later in the process. So, the science of chaos tells us, a butterfly may flap its wings in China and set in motion a chain of causes that affects a storm system in Boston. That is how interconnected everything is: we do a kind act, or speak angry words, or live in awareness, and the effects ripple out.

The more sensitive we are to the interdependence of things, the more we see how the quality of our own lives affects not only the people we actually meet but also all beings. The Buddha did something one night more than twenty-five hundred years ago under a tree in Bodh Gaya, India, and because of that act, you are sitting reading these words in the late twentieth century. How amazing! For this result to happen, a chain of events has spanned two and a half millennia and many different cultures and countries. And the chain does not end with you holding this book. It stretches from you through who knows what time and space.

In this mysterious universe of subtle and vast interconnections, each one of our actions is as delicate and far-reaching as the butterfly flapping its wings. And the freer we are from greed, hatred, and ignorance, the more our lives will be for the benefit of all. Reflecting on that fact can infuse our practice and our lives with spaciousness and love as we travel this ancient and fully contemporary path.

For More Information

Readers who desire information about Insight Meditation retreats and teaching worldwide may contact the Insight Meditation Society, 1230 Pleasant Street, Barre, Massachusetts 01005. For information about Insight Meditation audio and video cassette recordings, please contact the Dharma Seed Tape Library, Box 66, Wendell Depot, Massachusetts 01380.

Index

Index